AF251996

MANAGING STATE SOCIAL WORK

For Lydia, Seth and Vicky.

Managing State Social Work

Front-line management and the labour process perspective

JOHN HARRIS

Ashgate

Aldershot • Brookfield USA • Singapore • Sydney

Published by
Ashgate Publishing Ltd
Gower House
Croft Road
Aldershot
Hants GU11 3HR
England

Ashgate Publishing Company
Old Post Road
Brookfield
Vermont 05036
USA

British Library Cataloguing in Publication Data
Harris, John, 1952-
    Managing state social work : front-line management and the
    labour process perspective
    1.Social work administration - Great Britain
    I. Title
    361.3'068

Library of Congress Catalog Card Number: 97-78317

ISBN 1 85972 586 4

Printed in Great Britain by
Antony Rowe Ltd, Chippenham, Wiltshire

Contents

Figures and tables

Acknowledgements

Thanks are due in no small measure to: Mick Carpenter for displaying fortitude and endurance in nudging me along; Norma Baldwin and Hilary Graham for interest, support and covering my job at crucial points; Marcie Edwards for turning work round cheerfully and efficiently; my parents, who have always wanted to know how it was going; Vicky, Seth and Lydia for wholeheartedly supporting my efforts "to get it finished" and putting up with me and everything I let slide in the process.

Preface

The relationship between management and social welfare has only recently attracted sustained and critical attention. This book traces one aspect of that relationship, the management of state social work. In doing so, the focus is on the social work labour process, with particular reference to front-line management.

After considering the orthodox industrial model of the labour process, developed by Braverman and utilised by radical social work writers, the book proposes a bureau-professional model as an alternative. This bureau-professional model is tested through a small-scale case study of a local authority Social Services Department.

On the basis of the case study's findings, the conclusion reached is that the labour process perspective has a role to play as a critical paradigm employed in the analysis of developments in state social work.

1 Introduction

The relationship between management and social welfare has, somewhat belatedly, begun to attract sustained and critical attention (Pollitt 1990; Clarke et al 1994; Clarke and Newman 1997). This book tracks back the significance of the relationship between management and social work to the 1970s and early 1980s, the era in which 'management' entered the language of local authority social work. The focus is on the social work labour process, with particular reference to front-line management. The book's origins lie in the orthodox industrial model of the labour process developed by Braverman and utilised by adherents to the radical social work paradigm.

The radical social work paradigm

In the 1970s a loose-knit radical social work movement, containing a variety of Left hues (Clark and Asquith, 1975, pp. 105-106), pitted a socialist paradigm against the reformist social democratic paradigm which had dominated social work's development within the British post-war welfare state (Langan and Lee, 1989, p. 14; Langan, 1992, p. 2). Within the socialist paradigm, time-honoured social democratic assumptions were rejected as social work was scrutinised and recast. In an early contribution to this intellectual shift, Leonard analysed the wide-ranging nature of the change in approach which the socialist paradigm represented:

> Conceptualisations about social work are primarily social products and reflect the particular socio-economic base upon which social welfare institutions have grown...It is because of the power of the dominant ideological formulations of social work, and their implications in practice, that it is important to develop radical perspectives on practice... The systematic formulation of the objectives

and methods of radical practice is crucial. Such a formulation must distinguish clearly between the description of the present activities of social workers and the exploratory prescription of what activities might be undertaken by social workers within a radical paradigm (Leonard, 1975, p. 46).

The radical paradigm's demystification of existing social work, as envisaged by Leonard, was undertaken to a large extent by Marxist-influenced variants of sociology (Langan and Lee, 1989, p. 1; Langan, 1992, p. 2). In these variants of sociology, social work was attacked as a form of social control and located within the ideological functions of welfare in a capitalist state (Clarke 1979, pp. 125-126). As a consequence, the radical social work movement embraced class as the focal point of critical analysis (Hearn, 1982a, p. 22; Langan and Lee, 1989, pp. 9-10; Day, 1992, p. 12, p. 15; Langan, 1992, p. 2).

Although tensions existed between academics and practitioners within the radical social work paradigm, concerning the relationship between radical theory and radical forms of practice (Cohen, 1975; Clarke, 1979; Hearn, 1982a), the focus on social class ensured that tensions were less evident between academics and practitioners in the identification of social workers, first and foremost, as workers (Langan and Lee, 1989, p. 12). The underpinning of the radical paradigm by the theorists' analysis of social work as paid work was endorsed by the activism of practitioners in the work setting. Practitioners were enjoined to 'float like a butterfly and sting like a bee' in their employing organisations (Corrigan and Leonard, 1978, p.157). The proof of practitioners' radical credentials lay in the manifestation of an anti-management stance (Clarke, 1979, p. 131), with their agencies being regarded as 'just as big a problem as external factors' (Langan and Lee, 1989, p. 5).

The theoretical resource for the analysis of developments in social work as a job, and for on-the-job, anti-management activism within Social Services Departments, was Braverman's *Labor and Monopoly Capital* (1974). Braverman's book made a marked impact on the radical social work movement in the 1970s and early 1980s. It became the cornerstone of critiques developed by radical theorists and by radical social work activists in the 'Seebohm factories' (Simpkin, 1983, p. 17), a term used in this period to describe local authority Social Services Departments. Following the book's publication, social work was represented within the radical social work paradigm as a labour process embedded in an industrial model of intensified managerial control (see the discussion in Chapter Three). This became the analytical framework for understanding the labour process within and against which radical social work was to be created. Exploring the position of social workers, and the forces exerted to manage and control them, became an element of radical thought and action which was accorded at least as much importance as face-to-face work with service users. The issue of managerial control of social workers was seen as 'one of the key factors determining the nature of personal social services organisation and practice' (Jones, 1983, p. 131).

Front-line management

Although the position of social workers, and control over them, had become central to the radical social work paradigm's analysis, consideration of management and management processes was noticeably absent (Hearn and Jones, 1981). This absence was particularly noticeable in relation to front-line management and is puzzling for two reasons. First, if social work management was controlling the work of state social workers as part of an overall trend within capitalist Britain, the front-line manager's experience of, and implication in, these developments was likely to be a particularly pertinent vantage point from which to view them. Secondly, the front-line manager's own experience of managerial control was an area which had been skirted around in the radical social work texts. Working out from these two reasons to wider issues, four factors gave the book's particular focus on front-line management added impetus.

First, the public sector has been relatively neglected within the labour process perspective. Although a wave of case studies critical of the broad brush approach of orthodox earlier labour process contributions appeared in the 1980s (Crompton and Jones, 1984; Knights and Willmott, 1986a, 1986b; Knights, Willmott and Collinson, 1985; Wood, 1982, 1989), the appreciation that not all forms of work can be understood through a labour process perspective geared to explaining manual labour in capitalist industrial production was still in the process of gaining currency amongst labour process theorists in the 1990s (Thompson and McHugh, 1990, p. 42; Smith, Knights and Willmott, 1991, pp. 1-2). Dent reminded labour process theorists that the public sector is a 'critical case for labour process analysis, if only because of its historically necessary role within all capitalist societies, and to ignore it leaves labour process analysis seriously weakened' (Dent, 1991, p. 68). Social work in particular has been ignored by the labour process perspective except for the attention it received from radical social work writers, whose work was itself at a tangent from the general labour process literature.

Secondly, the neglect of the public sector in labour process analysis can be explained by the difficulties likely to be encountered in adapting Braverman's analysis to a labour process not engaged in manufacturing and/or the direct production of surplus value. Thirdly, the radical social work texts seemed not to have faced up to the difficulty of analysing the labour process of an occupation which retained at the least a degree of autonomy over the carrying out of its work. Fourthly, the study of the social work labour process in the radical literature paid little attention to either contextualising or researching the social work labour process.

The book

In addressing these factors, initially the book adopts a two-pronged approach. The first prong involves selectively summarising those aspects of the main debates within the general labour process literature which have a bearing on how the labour process perspective was applied to social work within the radical social work paradigm and then considering how the labour process perspective was utilised by radical writers. The second prong concerns seeing the context and culture of local authority Social Services Departments as critical in shaping the nature of the social work labour process. Therefore, the second prong is the development of a framework for analysing the social work labour process which is not grounded in the industrial model of the radical social work paradigm. These two prongs are pursued in the chapters which follow.

In Chapter Two the origins of the industrial model of the labour process are considered through an outline of Braverman's reworking of the legacy of Marx's approach in *Labor and Monopoly Capital*. Ensuing developments in the labour process perspective are pursued through a review of key themes identified in the considerable theoretical and empirical debate which followed the publication of *Labor and Monopoly Capital*. The four themes which are regarded as pertinent to the later consideration of front-line management in social work are: managerial control strategies; the indeterminacy of labour power; worker consent; and monolithic management. In Chapter Three, these themes are then transferred from their origins in the general labour process literature and put to use as the basis for evaluating the radical social work paradigm's representation of the social work labour process as having moved towards an industrial model which steadily encroached on the autonomy of front-line field social workers, through managers' wresting of control over their work. Chapter Four sets out an alternative approach to the social work labour process which takes account of the distinctive features of social work, as a state-mediated, bureau-professional labour process. Chapter Five fleshes out this bureau-professional model through consideration of the relatively autonomous levels of the social work labour process. Chapter Six introduces a small-scale case study of "Welfareville" Social Services Department and sets out the structure of the social work labour process. Data from the case study are used to test the bureau-professional model of the social work labour process against the orthodox Bravermanian model of the radical social work texts. The position of front-line managers in the labour process is considered through an examination of their identifications and commitments in relation to management (Chapter Seven) and trade unionism (Chapter Eight). Chapter Nine summarises the discussion of the earlier chapters and concludes with some implications for future work in this area.

2 The labour process perspective and management

Introduction

This chapter considers the distinguishing characteristics of the labour process perspective and debates within it. The chapter highlights key themes in the development of the perspective which have a bearing on the subsequent examination of the social work labour process and front-line management. It begins with the legacy of Marx, moves on to Braverman's 'rediscovery' of the labour process and then discusses the post-Braverman debate in relation to four themes: managerial control strategies; the indeterminacy of labour power; worker consent; and monolithic management. The chapter's exploration of these themes provides a baseline for evaluating, in the following chapter, the work of radical social work writers in advocating the application of the labour process perspective to social work, based on an industrial model.

The legacy of Marx

In *Capital Volume One*, Marx analyses changes in the nature of work under the capitalist mode of production. To begin with, Marx describes the features of the labour process in any social formation as ***purposeful activity*** combined with the deployment of ***instruments*** in order to produce ***use values*** from the object of labour. He sets out these three components of the labour process as follows:

> ***Purposeful activity:*** Labour is, first of all, a process between man (*sic*) and nature, a process by which man, through his own actions, mediates, regulates and controls the metabolism between himself and nature. He confronts the materials of nature as a force of nature...He acts upon external nature and changes it (Marx, 1974, p. 169).

Instruments: An instrument of labour is a thing, or a complex of things, which the worker interposes between himself and the object of labour and which serves as a conductor, directing his activity onto that object (Marx, 1974, p. 171).

Use Values: In the labour process, therefore, man's activity via the instruments of labour effects an alteration in the object of labour which was intended from the outset. The process is extinguished in the product. The product of the process is a use value, a piece of natural material adapted to human needs by means of a change in its form (Marx, 1974, p. 173).

Marx argues that these three components are the essential features of the labour process. He then develops the discussion of the labour process in general into a consideration of the particular form of the labour process under the capitalist mode of production by stressing two distinctive features of the capitalist labour process: first, 'the worker works under the control of the capitalist to whom his labour belongs' (Marx, 1974, p. 178); secondly, 'the product of the worker's labour is appropriated by the capitalist in order to realise surplus value' (Marx, 1974, p. 178), a process which Marx refers to as the 'valorisation process' (Marx, 1974, p. 179). It is this combination of control of the labour process and the realisation of surplus value which, Marx argues, characterises the capitalist production process: 'The production process, considered as the unity of the labour process and the process of valorisation, is the capitalist process of production, or the capitalist form of production of commodities' (Marx, 1974, p. 192).

Marx does not suggest that the purchase of labour power by the capitalist is in itself sufficient to ensure that labour is appropriated. The capitalist is engaged in the control of the labour process in order to maximise the potential for labour which the worker brings to the labour process and by so doing to realise surplus value. In Marx's terms, labour power is 'variable capital' (Marx, 1974, p. 205): 'I use the term labour power or capacity for labour to denote the aggregate of mental and physical capabilities existing in a human being' (Marx, 1974, p. 154). As variable capital, labour power has to be transformed into labour: 'The use of labour power is labour itself. The purchaser of labour consumes it by setting the seller of it to work. By working the latter becomes in actuality what previously he only was potentially, namely labour power in action, a worker' (Marx, 1974, p. 169). Hence, control of labour power is necessary to the capitalist in order to ensure that its nature as variable capital is rendered susceptible to the maximisation of surplus value.

Marx's original formulation of the labour process in *Capital Volume One* became the starting point for the development of the labour process perspective in the work of Braverman.

Braverman and the rediscovery of the labour process

It might have been anticipated that Marx's analysis of the labour process would have been reconsidered as capitalism developed but this was not so. Indeed, at the beginning of *Labor and Monopoly Capital* Braverman claims that no comprehensive Marxist analysis of the labour process had taken place since Marx's original formulation of it (Braverman, 1974, p. 9). Braverman's explanation for the absence of a reconsideration of the labour process (Braverman, 1974, pp. 9-13), and Thompson's elaboration of it (Thompson, 1983, pp. 58-64), rely on two factors. The first factor is the institutional boundary in the West between trade unions at the work place and wider working class politics, a boundary which mirrors Marx's neglect of political struggle in his discussion of the labour process. The second factor was the adoption of the techniques of scientific management by the then Eastern bloc. By suggesting that scientific management could be used for different ends, namely the creation of material resources in a society's economic base for the extension of socialism, the techniques themselves, Braverman argues, were presented as neutral.

Braverman's work is an attempt to fill analytical void following Marx's analysis of the labour process. In so doing, Braverman counters the apparent political neutrality of scientific management techniques and their appropriation by the then state socialist regimes. His thesis is that the management of the labour process is being moulded in a direct way by the demands of capitalism in order to appropriate surplus value through the deliberate control of labour (Braverman, 1974, p.121).

Braverman's thesis begins from a review of Marx's theory of the labour process in the context of a detailed examination of changes in the organisation of production under monopoly capitalism. In a restatement and reaffirmation of Marx's theory (Braverman, 1974, chs. 1-3), Braverman emphasises the need to take the nature and purpose of production under capitalism into account when analysing the conditions of work. He sees the design of jobs, the division of labour and work organisation all as underpinned by the motive of accumulating capital through the extraction of surplus value. It is the logic of capital accumulation that is regarded as dictating the organisation of work, allowing the labour process to be understood through an appreciation of its capitalist origins and its embodiment of the fundamental antagonism between capitalist and workers. This conflict, and in particular the employers' need to maximise profits, dictates the necessity for a management-initiated strategy to wrest control of the labour process from workers. As a part of this strategy the scope for workers' control of, and discretion in, work has to be severely limited.

In specifying this management-initiated strategy, Braverman argues that in monopoly capitalism the necessity for capital to realise the potential of labour power contains interlinked tendencies towards the de-skilling of the workforce in a different kind and scope of capitalist control through the division of labour. The design of the labour process is fragmented into smaller, less skilled tasks which are more susceptible to co-ordination and control. As a result, only managers have an overall grasp of the labour process:

> Workers who are controlled only by general orders and discipline are not adequately controlled, because they retain their grip on the actual processes of labour...To change this situation control over the labour process must pass into the hands of management...by the control and dictation of each step of the process, including its performance (Braverman, 1974, p. 100).

Braverman describes management appropriation of control over the labour process in terms of the separation of the processes of conception and execution. Thus, the establishment and maintenance of managerial control is central to Braverman's analysis. Braverman sees the twentieth century as bringing about the subordination of labour through the redesigning of jobs and control over the organisation of work. The essence of scientific management - or 'Taylorism' - is the separation of planning how to do a job from the doing of it. As execution has become increasingly separated from conception, the bulk of employees are involved in simple mundane tasks. Freedom and discretion are removed from the shop floor and became the monopoly of management. For Braverman scientific management is the pervasive, driving force of the monopoly capitalist era. It is the means by which capitalist production had been systematised. Braverman sums up Taylorism as follows: '...the first principle is the gathering together and development of knowledge of the labour process, and the second is the concentration of this knowledge as the exclusive preserve of management - together with its converse, the absence of such knowledge among workers - then the third step is the use of this monopoly of knowledge to control each step of the labour process and its mode of execution' (Braverman, 1974, p. 119).

As is apparent, for Braverman this universal trend towards increased managerial control, leading to managerial domination of the labour process, is the hallmark of the nature of work under monopoly capitalism. The manager is presented as having 'uncontested, unilateral control' (Zimbalist, 1979, p. xii). Giddens sums up Braverman's work: 'Braverman's analysis...suggests that the draining off upwards of control of the labour task from the worker is a progressive (and also seemingly irresistible) process in the technological development of modern capitalism' (Giddens, 1979, p. 146).

Although Braverman's Labour and Monopoly Capital discusses developments in the organisation of work in the United States, his analysis seen as broadly applicable to capitalist countries which developed in broadly similar directions, such as Britain, and it acted as the framework for a huge expansion in subsequent research. As a result of Braverman's work, from 1974 onwards the debate about the control of the labour process occupied a central position in the study of work, both in terms of the development of the capitalist labour process in general (Friedman, 1977; Edwards, 1979; Burawoy, 1979) and also in relation to particular issues and case studies (Gorz, 1976; Zimbalist, 1979; Berg, 1979; Nichols, 1980; Wood, 1982). Conflicting positions emerged. For example, the case studies edited by Zimbalist are used by him to support the orthodox Bravermanian model, whilst Wood's volume brings together critical accounts of the extent and consequences of de-skilling. Nevertheless, the origins of a wide-ranging literature lay in Braverman's reconsideration of the labour process. The labour process thesis enabled researchers to link together subjects previously treated in isolation in fields such as industrial sociology, organisational studies and industrial relations. The thesis provoked extensive theoretical discussion and generated a mountain of empirical data. Thus the study of work owes an enormous debt to Braverman's pioneering analysis. However, the debate which followed the publication of Labour and Monopoly Capital reveals that Braverman's analysis was, inevitably, only a partial understanding of the complexities of the labour process.

Any attempt to categorise the wide-ranging post-Braverman debate is somewhat artificial.   In anticipation of the subsequent consideration of the social work labour process, the key questions which are considered to be relevant to the social work labour process are injected into this debate:

- Does management always choose the same strategy?
- Is labour readily susceptible to managerial domination?
- Does labour always have to be actively controlled by management?
- Is management a unified coherent interest?

For the purpose of responding to these questions, the discussion which follows addresses four themes, all of which combine to undermine the determinism of Braverman's model.   First, Braverman is criticised on the grounds that it can be established empirically that in dealing with labour a variety of managerial control strategies exist.   Secondly, it is argued that Braverman fails to appreciate 'the central indeterminacy of labour potential' (Littler, 1982, p. 31) and as a consequence neglects the difficulties involved in transforming labour power into actual labour. Thirdly, consideration is given to worker consent as an alternative to managerial control.   Fourthly, Braverman's assumption that management is a monolithic interest is challenged.   These four themes are considered in turn in order to shed light on the questions injected into the post-Braverman debate.

Managerial control strategies: does management always choose the same strategy?

A more flexible approach to the labour process which allows for the use of a variety of managerial control strategies, rather than assuming an imperative towards the exclusive reliance on the techniques of scientific management, emerged in the post-Braverman debate. Some writers (Friedman, 1977a; Edwards, 1979; Littler, 1982; Wood, 1982) reject the rigidity of Braverman's elevation of scientific management as *the* managerial control strategy. Edwards, for example, argues that in early capitalism, or 'competitive capitalism', the control of work took place under the direct supervision of the capitalist but then, as the size of workforces grew, with the expansion of production and its increasing complexity, the personal ties between the capitalist and workers were eroded and worker resistance intensified. Edwards regards these factors as responsible for the development of systematic approaches to management of which Taylorism is considered to be simply one variant (Edwards, 1979, pp. 25-26). Friedman takes a similar position: 'Taylorian scientific management is not the only strategy for exercising managerial authority and, given the reality of worker resistance, often it is not the most appropriate' (Friedman, 1977a, p. 80). Burawoy notes the difficulty of identifying an over-arching capitalist control strategy present in such a diverse range of enterprises as crafts, domestic industry, sub-contracting and large-scale manufacture (Burawoy, 1981, pp. 96-97). Even when Taylorist methods are employed, Edwards points out that their failure to secure worker participation has costs. Workers' resistance, and in some cases sabotage, leads to restrictions in output (Edwards, 1979, p. 99).

Friedman and Edwards examine specific managerial control strategies which they regard as alternatives to Taylorian scientific management. Friedman makes a distinction between workers who are subject to 'direct control' and those who enjoy a position of 'responsible autonomy' (Friedman, 1977a). He traces back the over-emphasis on direct control to Braverman's neglect of worker resistance and the glossing over of a contradiction in the labour process. From a Marxist perspective, this contradiction centres around the potential of labour to be self-directing and its location within antagonistic relations of production. Friedman argues that managers can attempt to contain this contradiction either through direct control or through harnessing labour's potential for self-direction. He identifies management's accommodation to both worker resistance and market pressures as the backcloth to the choice of managerial control strategies. Friedman distinguishes between 'central' workers, whose skill is vital to the maintenance of long-term profitability, and 'peripheral' workers. Whilst peripheral workers can be subjected to 'direct control' because their skills are easily replaceable, central workers are granted 'responsible autonomy' which involves 'the maintenance of managerial authority by getting workers to identify with the competitive aims of the enterprise so that they will act "responsibly" with the minimum of supervision' (Friedman, 1977a, p. 48). Friedman's case study of the 'gang system' in the car industry, which serves as an example of a responsible autonomy strategy, highlights arrangements negotiated between management and central workers concerning working methods.

Friedman's work adds weight to the necessity of addressing the issues of variation in control strategies but his view of management choosing from two strategies of control runs the risk of perpetuating a view of management as all-encompassing, proactive and pre-emptive; the risk of 'collapsing management's potentially wide-ranging repertoire of practices into essentially two' (Nichols, 1980, p, 276). Coombs (1978) and Crompton and Reid (1982) question the setting of one technique against another as alternatives and stress combinations of controls available to management.

Edwards' historical study of the United States is wider in scope than Friedman's analysis. Edwards locates the capitalist labour process in the 'contested terrain' of workplace conflict and the economic contradictions of a company's operations. He sets out an historical succession in managerial control strategies which changed as a result of 'the continuing contention of classes' (Edwards, 1979, p. viii). He argues that managerial control has shifted from the initial reliance on the 'simple control' of capitalists themselves under 'competitive capitalism' through 'technical control' to 'bureaucratic control'. He contends that the collapse of 'simple control', under the pressures of class struggle and the centralisation of capital, led to structural forms of control which are located in the physical and social structure of the workplace rather than in the personal presence and authority of the capitalist. The first of these structural strategies, 'technical control', relies on the use of mechanisation to plan the flow of work in order to minimise the problem of transforming labour power into labour (Edwards, 1979, p. 112) and is typified by the assembly line. In contrast, 'bureaucratic control' relies on the organisational and social structure of the enterprise and takes the forms of systematic hierarchical command, stratification of work into job categories, impersonal rules, promotion opportunities, career planning and formal definitions of responsibility (Edwards, 1979, p. 131).

Edwards' concept of bureaucratic control can be supported from several quarters. Stinchcombe (1965) and Brown (1982) direct particular attention to the subjective component of careers and the internalised control exerted by 'career consciousness' (Stinchcombe, 1965, p. 35). In addition, bureaucratic organisations can be analysed as the embodiment of the arrangements made to control work. (For summaries, see Salaman, 1979, pp. 102-142; Clegg and Dunkerley, 1980, Ch. 13). Littler (1982) and Nichols and Beynon (1977) point to controlling features of the bureaucratic employment relationship, such as the lack of alternative employment in local labour markets and overall unemployment levels, as being likely to lead to greater acceptance of managerial control unless some form of protection exists, for example from a trade union, which offers the possibility of organising opposition. This literature, taken together with Edwards' work, offers more detailed consideration of managerial control strategies but also begins to undermine Edwards' formulation.

Although Edwards accepts that all three forms of control he identifies continue to exist, he maintains that a process of historical succession takes place: 'each form of control corresponds to a definite stage in the development of the most important representative firms' (Edwards, 1979, p. 21). As with Friedman, this distinction between alternative forms of control is problematic. In Edwards' work this is compounded by his insistence on their essentially sequential character. Nevertheless, the combination of Edwards' emphasis on different managerial control strategies at different stages of capitalism and Friedman's identification of different strategies for different groups of workers is clearly an improvement on Braverman in conceptualising the control of the labour process. As classifications of variations in forms of control, they counter the rigidity of Braverman's one-dimensional, unilinear perspective. However, they were still somewhat abstracted accounts which rest on the assumption that management has a grand design (Hill, 1981, p. 99).

Child warns against heavy reliance on a view of management as the exercise of 'strategic choice' (Child, 1985). His warning suggests the necessity of guarding against the temptation to reject Braverman's insistence on scientific management as *the* form of control in favour of more sophisticated accounts of the control process which themselves may share with Braverman some of the weaknesses encountered in trying to ossify a dynamic process.

In retrospect, the pre-eminence accorded by Braverman to Taylorism as a set of techniques, may be less important than Taylorism's ideological function as the legitimisation of systematic approaches to management in general (Burawoy, 1978, pp. 276-281). In this regard, other writers go beyond the classification of alternatives to Taylorian scientific management and argue that the recurring emphasis on managerial control may not always be an appropriate starting point. Storey suggests the possibility of middle-range management initiatives which he places between 'grand strategy' and 'muddling through' (Storey, 1985, p. 202). Littler and Salaman contend that 'control only becomes an issue when profitability is threatened' (Littler and Salaman, 1982, p. 265). However, simply to turn the spotlight away from control and on to the valorisation process does not indicate either how control will be exercised in specific circumstances or how any conflict between short-term profitability and long-term prospects will be resolved. Nevertheless, the possibility that 'the first priority is accumulation not control' (Salaman, and Littler, 1982, p. 64) breaks the stranglehold that managerial control has had on the discussion so far. Another strand of critical comment on the presumed supremacy of managerial control comes from a focus on the indeterminacy of labour power.

The indeterminacy of labour power: is labour readily susceptible to managerial domination?

Although Braverman acknowledges the importance of the distinction between labour and labour power at the outset of his argument and, following Marx, this distinction forms the basis of his thesis concerning the capitalist imperative to control the labour process (Braverman, 1974, pp. 45-48), he puts it to one side in his subsequent analysis. His work conveys the impression that 'the domination of labour by capital within the labour process is virtually complete' (Coombs, 1978, p. 94). However, as we saw in the earlier section on Marx, the purchase of labour power involves the purchase of physical and mental *capacities*. Those capacities have to be put to work in order to be realised as actual labour. Labour power is variable capital not just in an economic sense, but in the variability represented by the relative strength of participants in the production process (Nichols, 1980, p. 35). Braverman's one-dimensional view of managerial control can be depicted as a scenario in which 'neither workers nor managers play any conscious part either in the mediation of the relationship between the control and organisation of the labour process and the imperatives of capitalism, or in the development and acting out of struggles and negotiations' (Littler and Salaman, 1982, p. 253).

The lack of attention to workers' struggles in Braverman's work is remedied by writers highlighting resistance as a potentially problematic property of labour power for the manager (Coombe, 1978; Stark, 1980; Elger, 1982). Burawoy, for example, contends on the basis of his research that it is more common for management to react to worker resistance than to consciously pre-plan strategies of control (Burawoy, 1979, pp. 180-183). This aspect of the indeterminacy of labour power can be illustrated by studies of variations in worker resistance historically, by variations in worker resistance between groups of workers and by variations across different societies (Friedman, 1977b; Littler, 1982; Gospel and Littler, 1983; Cousins, 1987, Ch. 6). These richly detailed illustrations of worker resistance are in stark contrast to Braverman's treatment of resistance which consists of a single reference to the 'storm of opposition among trade unions' to Taylorism (Braverman, 1974, p. 130).

Worker consent: does labour always have to be actively controlled by management?

Attention to the indeterminacy of labour power, the continual problem of realising its potential in the context of worker resistance, and variation in control strategies has so far left to one side another feature of the labour process: the possibility of consent, or at least compliance, on the part of workers - a feature which has been relatively neglected in the search for evidence of worker resistance to counter the excesses of Braverman's analysis.

Prior to Braverman's work, Beynon (1973) identified an important component in fostering workers' co-operation. He argues that the overall role of management as a separate function and the legitimacy of this role has to be established as a precondition for the development of specific managerial strategies to control the labour process. Whilst Beynon's argument is that this suggests two components of control - at least a minimum level of acceptance of managerial authority plus specific methods of control in order to realise labour power as actual labour - the greater the extent to which workers consent to managerial authority presumably the greater the possibility of reduction in the use of specific methods of control. The legitimacy of management could conceivably become sufficient in itself rather than being only a necessary precondition to the introduction of specific forms of control. In any event instances of resistance and negotiation will be played out against the backcloth of the legitimacy of managerial authority and may represent the re-negotiation of consent.

Cressey and MacInnes (1980) argue that even if control strategies are being consciously implemented, managers still have to 'surrender the means of production to the 'control' of workers for their actual use in the production process'. They conclude that managers 'must to some degree seek a co-operative relation' with workers (Cressey and MacInnes, 1980, p. 14). They consider the possibility of managers stimulating motivation in order to harness the potential of labour power and point to workers' interests in maintaining the viability of the enterprise which employs them. (Similarly, Buchanan (1986) contends that workers have a stake in ensuring their firm's survival.) This view raises the possibility that active involvement of workers, rather than their subjugation as objects of control, may be both possible and in an employer's interests. Management may value the use of co-operative labour.

Burawoy develops the most sustained analysis of consent. He argues for the need to scrutinise ideological processes at the workplace and to pay attention to 'the engineering of consent rather than the imposition of control'. He points to Marx's omission of consent in his formulation of the labour process and demonstrates the way in which playing 'games' - the 'making out' of the industrial sociology literature - implies consent to the rules (Burawoy, 1979, p. 73). Burawoy's other main concern, with bureaucratic features of the workplace rather than coercion, echoes Edwards' (1979) analysis of bureaucratic control but Burawoy goes further. He argues that industrial enterprises are best understood as internal labour markets characterised by competitive individualism and commitment to the enterprise, with the worker seen as a consenting industrial 'citizen' whose rights are safeguarded by an internal 'state'.

Burawoy's work balances the preoccupation of other writers with control. He may exaggerate the extent of the shift from 'despotic' to 'hegemonic' forms of management (Burawoy, 1979, p. 1985) but, in the process, he raises the importance of considering structures of consent as well as strategies of control in any attempt to analyse the labour process. His work points up the fact that the relationship between employer and employee involves both conflict and co-operation. There is an essential tension for management 'between the need to regulate and dominate the production process versus the need to maximise the creativity and reliability of labour' (Littler and Salaman, 1984, p. 90). In contrast, Braverman adopts an orthodox Marxist perspective in which he depicts consciousness as gradually changing, without specifying the processes involved and with no reference to subjective experiences at the workplace, until 'a large proletariat in new form' (Braverman, 1974, p. 355) emerged fully formed.

The final element to be discussed in the post-Braverman debate is the questioning of Braverman's assumption of the existence of a monolithic management interest.

Monolithic management: is management a unified coherent interest?

The tempering of Braverman's model undertaken thus far (-by uncovering more sophisticated and subtle accounts of managerial control strategies, by drawing attention to the indeterminacy of labour power and by elaborating processes of workers' consent-) could still allow the possibility of a unified and coherent management interest. Thus far, the discussion has set to one side the possibility of divisions within management in its use of 'management' as a generic term.

Storey cautions against regarding management as monolithic in arguing that only the most general objectives concerning an enterprise's survival may unite managers. He suggests that 'in reality much (of managerial action) is misguided, self-interested, half-hearted, short-term and inchoate' (Storey, 1986, p. 49). Rose and Jones, in a study of six industrial organisations, found that management strategy was 'piecemeal uncoordinated and empiricist' (Rose and Jones, 1985, p. 137). A glance sideways at the literature from the sociology of organisations reveals that organisations have multiple goals which are often difficult to locate, are frequently in conflict and may vary over time (Silverman, 1970; Perrow, 1970). Such views of managerial activity open up the possibility of management being 'fissured, both vertically and horizontally' (Storey, 1986, p. 49). This can be illustrated by comparing the position and interests of managers who formulate policy and allocate resources with those front-line managers who implement policy and vet applications for resources. Littler makes the point that the latter group of managers have to interpret rules and apply procedures and that the ways in which such tasks are accomplished in practice vary from the intentions of senior managers (Littler, 1982, pp. 49-52). Managers can also resist policy or not understand it (Wood and Kelly, 1982). In this respect, Burawoy notes that an understanding of the inter-relationships between different factions of management is essential in order to comprehend management activity (Burawoy, 1979, p. 182).

In contrast Braverman, throughout *Labor and Monopoly Capital*, stresses the advantageous position of management as an undifferentiated whole in a way which is at odds with later work stressing the possible diversity of managerial activity and interests. However, he makes one comment which suggests the possibility of a more complex analysis: 'Management has become administration, which is a labour process conducted for the purpose of control within the corporation and conducted moreover as a labour process exactly analogous to the process of production, although it produces no product other than the operation and co-ordination of the corporation' (Braverman, 1974, p. 267). Braverman's comment is an intriguing aside to his tendency to present management as monolithic and homogeneous, performing a corporate control function over workers. Light can be shed on Braverman's aside by the work of Neo-Marxist theorists who have developed analyses of the class structure, within which relations of production in the labour process are located, through the identification of an intermediate stratum between capital and labour. This stratum has been presented in the guises of 'the new middle class' (Carchedi, 1977) or 'the service class' (Abercrombie and Urry, 1983).

Carchedi's account contains the most developed analysis of the impact on the labour process of positing the existence of an intermediate class stratum. Carchedi argues that the labour process has become increasingly complex and identifies the key to its complexity as lying in its collective nature which has led to the emergence of 'an ensemble of people organised as a collective labourer' (Carchedi, 1977, p. 58). He also identifies the emergence of 'the global capitalist'. The role of the capitalist has been sub-divided so that the functions associated with the appropriation of surplus value are also collectivised (Carchedi, 1977, p. 68). Carchedi identifies managerial levels which have a contradictory location in performing the functions of both the collective worker and the global functions of capital and terms those who occupy these levels, 'the new middle class' (Carchedi, 1977, p. 92).

Crompton and Jones (1984) echo Carchedi's analysis and reject the 'spurious homogeneity' bestowed on the intermediate stratum by service class theorists. They argue that much of the service class is located in a 'structurally ambiguous' category, carrying out to varying degrees the functions of both capital and labour with concrete examination of given circumstances and constraints which shape responses being required (Crompton and Jones, 1984, pp. 223-224). Ramsay et al. suggest similarly that Carchedi's analysis remains abstracted from empirical investigation of attitudes and behaviour in areas of structural ambiguity. They contend that attitudes and behaviour cannot be deduced, a priori, from Carchedi's analytical framework. They call for more detailed examination of experiences, identity and actions (Ramsay et al., 1991, pp. 36-37).

The contradictory location of some managers in structurally ambiguous positions in the labour process is elaborated by Teulings (1986). Working from Braverman's comment on management as a labour process, referred to above, Teulings notes that the implication is that management can also be subject to processes of fragmentation and control (Teulings, 1986, p. 143; and see Cousins, 1987, p. 46). Teulings makes the case for a 'differentiated management with separate rationalities' (Teulings, 1986, p. 144). He suggests that differentiation of management into institutional, strategic, structuring and operational levels produces several management labour processes: '...the differentiation of management function not only takes the form of a vertical division between levels of management but also produces a relative autonomy of rationalities or logics of action at each level...There is no unique or common reference point for all levels to which all actions can be orientated' (Teulings, 1986, pp. 157-159). Teulings gives an example of the possibility of alliances between operational workers and lower managers (Teuling, 1986, p. 143). He argues that the divisions and differences between levels of management stem from two motives: the opportunity to preserve or increase managerial power and the defence of group interests (Teulings, 1986, p. 160). He considers that the imbalance between different levels of management leads to negotiation between the different levels being an increasing feature of work organisations (Teulings, 1986, pp. 160-164). He identifies feelings of powerlessness on the part of individual managers 'for the rules which led to success in his (*sic*) own labour process no longer appeared to apply, and no longer appeared to work in the process of accommodation with other logics of action. The power of the individual manager (and, in particular, a sense of power) thus lags behind the power of management. The manager forms part of an extensive machinery of power without being able to derive from it any real sense of sharing that power' (Teulings, 1986, pp. 164-165).

Teulings' stress on the 'relative autonomy of rationalities or logics of action' at each level is illustrated in a study of the then National Coal Board by Hopper et al. (Hopper et al., 1986). They discovered dislocated managerial relationships between headquarters, the area structure and the collieries which contained contradictions between corporate strategies and operational concerns. Resistance to managerial practices and 'managerial desires for autonomy were significant' (Hopper et al., 1986, p. 126). Buchanan also stresses that decision-making by managers cannot be regarded as straightforward unanimity with a corporate managerial interest: 'The decisions which determine the organisation and control of the labour process are made and influenced by middle and junior managers...and serve a range of objectives, related to personal careers as well as corporate policy' (Buchanan, 1986, p. 68). In similar vein, Storey notes that 'middle and lower level managers have their own position as employees to protect and this may well undermine their unambiguous devotion' (Storey, 1986, p. 49).

The implications of challenging the presentation in labour process theory of management as monolithic are first, that both the extent to which there are managerial strategies of control and the extent to which they are implemented has to be determined empirically. Implementation of a control strategy cannot be simply inferred from the articulation by senior managers of its existence. Secondly, a rigid and exclusive reliance on the explanatory power of a structural conflict of interests between all managers and all workers is unhelpful in elaborating potential diversity in the labour process. Instead, consideration needs to be given to how interests are defined, whether they are acted upon, individually or collectively, and how they are interpreted and reinterpreted on a day-to-day basis. A more fluid approach to interest definition would counsel against the study of the labour process beginning from assumptions about the crushing control of monolithic management: 'Management practice should be analysed as having the potential for compromise and consensus as well as conflict' (Littler and Salaman,

1982, p. 253). Thirdly, there may be more ambiguity in the position and practice of individual managers, particularly at the front-line level, than many writers working within the labour process perspective have suggested.

Conclusion

The accumulated criticisms of Braverman's work, following the publication of *Labor and Monopoly Capital*, undermined his model of a direct relationship between the continued appropriation of surplus value and an imperative towards scientific management as *the* form of managerial control. Rather, the injection of questions into the post-Braverman debate has indicated that: management does not always choose the same strategy; labour is not necessarily susceptible to managerial domination; labour does not always have to be actively controlled by management; and management is unlikely to be a unified, coherent interest.

As we have seen, the injection of questions into the post-Braverman debate uncovered criticisms centred around first, the existence of variation in managerial control strategies; secondly, the continual problem of transforming labour power into labour, evidenced by worker resistance; thirdly, the possibility of worker consent; fourthly, the elaboration of differentiation within management. As a result of the accumulation of these criticisms, within the labour process perspective the focus has shifted increasingly to analysis of the labour process as contested/ consenting terrain. For Storey the considerable weight of evidence from empirical studies suggests the existence of complexity and diversity in the labour process rather than the crushing uniformity presented in the work of early labour process writers. He argues that 'inherent contradictions (in the labour process) undermine any ultimate or absolute logic in the means of control' (Storey, 1985, p. 195). If Storey's argument is accepted, it suggests that what is needed is an approach to the study of labour processes which first, recognises their heterogeneity and second, can accommodate both structure and process. Such an approach would combine an analysis of the organisational structures of specific labour processes and the work processes through which the structures function. Analysis would proceed on the basis of empirical studies which developed the labour process perspective in specific contexts.

In the next chapter local authority social work as the location of a specific labour process is explored through the radical social work literature. The radical social work literature is discussed in relation to the key themes from the post-Braverman debate identified in this chapter and measured against the type of analysis which this chapter has suggested is likely to be most fruitful in the light of the criticisms of Braverman's original formulation of the labour process.

3 Managing state social work: towards an industrial model of the labour process?

The accumulated effect of the [Seebohm] re-organisation upon social workers was little dissimilar from the introduction of the assembly line by Henry Ford (Simpkin, 1983, p. 19).

Introduction

Although Braverman regards the level of state welfare expenditure as 'an arena for political agitation' (Braverman, 1974, pp. 286-7), he does not consider the nature of the labour process within state welfare sectors. The review of four key themes from the labour process literature in Chapter Two demonstrated the continued omission from the post-Braverman labour process perspective of systematic consideration of state welfare employment. The omission of state welfare employment in general, and social work in particular, from the labour process perspective needs to be rectified if we are to move on to consider front-line management in the social work labour process. The literature which begins to address the omission of social work from the labour process perspective is contained in a body of writing which emerged from within the 'radical social work' paradigm. The radical social work literature's account of the social work labour process, and an assessment of the extent to which this account keys into the post-Braverman refinement of the labour process perspective, is the subject of this chapter.

The chapter begins with the emergence of the radical social work paradigm. The themes used to structure the discussion of the post-Braverman debate on the labour process in Chapter Two are then revisited in relation to the radical social work literature's account of the social work labour process.

The radical social work paradigm

As was noted in Chapter One, in the 1970s the 'radical social work' paradigm was pitted against the social democratic paradigm which had dominated social work within the post-war welfare state. As the position of social workers and the forces exerted to manage and control them moved into prominence, following publication of Braverman's *Labour and Monopoly Capital,* Braverman's thesis filled a theoretical vacuum in the paradigm's consideration of the workplace of social work. The radical social work paradigm represented the social work labour process as being embedded in an industrial model.

In summary, the argument which united the small body of radical social work writers who drew on the labour process perspective (Bolger et al., 1981; Simpkin, 1979, 1983; Jones, 1983) was that the social work labour process had moved, and was still moving, towards an industrial model. In such a formulation of the social work labour process Social Services Departments - or 'Seebohm factories' (Simpkin, 1983, p. 17) - were presented as characterised by organisational forms which had steadily allowed the autonomy of front-line field social workers to be eroded, through managers' wresting of control over their work. Radical social work writers pointed to control being exercised over social work through an increasing division between the processes of conception (management) and execution (social worker), a division which had resulted in management becoming more powerful and front-line field social workers falling under their control. They stressed the importance of field social workers resisting these trends.

The radical social work paradigm's representation of the labour process is now discussed in more detail in relation to the themes identified in Chapter Two from the post-Braverman debate:

- Managerial control strategies;
- The indeterminacy of labour power;
- Worker consent;
- Monolithic management.

Managerial control strategies: does management always choose the same strategy?

Central to the radical social work writers' analysis of managerial control strategies was an orthodox Bravermanian approach to the separation of execution from conception. Bolger et al. consider that Braverman's concept has:

> ...a direct, central and biting relevance to welfare work. The Seebohm Departments...have increased their hierarchy and their authoritarian nature...this form has been directly lifted from the private enterprise arena

where its main aim has been to increase control by a central management team...the split is about knowledge of the whole process involved in the work. Some people have to carry out the work of the organisation and others plan it (Bolger et al., 1981, pp. 65-66).

The imperative to gain control over the planning of social work is considered to have resulted in the adoption of sophisticated management techniques which reduced the day-to-day autonomy of social workers: '...there is no doubt that this increasing sophistication has assumed a greater and greater control over the day-to-day caring process' (Bolger, 1981, p. 66). They identify a 'powerful de-skilling process' at work (Bolger et al., 1981, p. 68) in an overall tendency to adopt centralised and hierarchical modes of management found in capitalist enterprises: 'Control and cheapness of service provision were taken from capitalist enterprise and directly imposed on local government structures' (Bolger et al., 1981, p. 57). The end result, they argue, is that social workers have 'an individualised, de-skilled, hierarchical experience' of work (Bolger et al., 1981, p. 69).

In similar vein to Bolger et al., Jones identifies the control of social workers as one of the key factors determining the nature of organisation and practice in the personal social services (Jones, 1983, p. 131). He stresses the encroachment on field social workers' autonomy which the Seebohm reorganisation has brought about: 'The restructuring of the social services had a profound effect on social workers themselves. The bureaucratisation of Social Services Departments following the 1970 Local Authority Social Services Act has placed many extra constraints on social workers and greatly reduced the extent of their autonomy and control' (Jones, 1983, p. 113). Jones depicts Social Services Departments as complex and unresponsive bureaucratic organisations with long and hierarchical command structures which involve social workers in time-consuming form-filling and which have significantly reduced their control over direct work with service users (Jones, 1983, pp. 3-5):

> Even if one takes a most cursory overview of the recent history of social work, one feature that stands out is the extent to which controls have been introduced for governing the activities and work of social workers. The range of measures has been wide and varied, and has included large-scale changes in the organisation of Social Services Departments, with their expanded bureaucratic management hierarchies, more direct supervision over the social worker, and an expanded array of work processes which attempt to direct and regulate the social worker's contact with clients (Jones, 1983, p. 94).

He concludes that '...the Seebohm reorganisation has led to many social workers experiencing a marked diminution in their independence and far greater pressure to meet the requirements of their departments' (Jones, 1983, p. 114).

As a consequence of these pressures Social Services Departments are seen as requiring social workers who will 'obey the instructions of managers' (Jones, 1983, p. 113). Jones quotes Leonard concerning the development of 'a central administrative structure which ensures that the activities of the members of the organisation are all directed towards the official objectives' (Leonard, in Jones 1983, p. 114). The increasing removal of conception from the locus of execution in social work practice is regarded as bringing managerially-imposed requirements on field social workers and social workers' own professional objectives into conflict (Jones, 1983, p. 112). There is:

> ...a gradual process of change which appears to be slowly ensuring greater employer control over the majority of social services workers...In the main the major thrust of these changes appears to be in the direction of reducing further the already limited professional autonomy of social workers by introducing measures which will ensure more effective worker conformity to the policies of the employing agency. Such a process is by no means peculiar to social work, and writers such as Braverman have identified a similar process at work across the labour market, particularly in areas of skilled labour. The name given to the developments is that of 'proletarianisation'. For many social workers proletarianisation has become an increasing feature of their experience of work within a local authority Social Services Department, especially as a consequence of increasing bureaucratic controls over their work (Jones, 1983, p. 122).

In Jones' account the end result is that social workers are no longer able to practice casework (Jones, 1983, p. 115) because of the erosion by managers of the importance attached to the therapeutic relationship (Jones, 1983, pp. 118, 147).

In understanding such centralising developments, Simpkin's analysis points in a similar direction. He argues that social work is 'not immune from the business process... When the development of Social Services Departments is looked on as a whole, and in context, many of their present day features can be seen as part of a more general process affecting the whole world of work' (Simpkin, 1983, p. 93). In pursuing the argument he adopts a more extreme stance, through a direct analogy with the industrial sphere: 'The cumulative effect of the [Seebohm] reorganisation upon social workers was little dissimilar from the introduction of the assembly line by Henry Ford...From being a craft motor engineering had become the repetition of a detailed operation...workers...found that the same mode of production had encroached on every sphere of production' (Simpkin, 1983, p. 19). Simpkin contends that social workers should be regarded as members of a new proletariat '...as ever tighter control is exerted over their work processes' (Simpkin, 1983, p. 94). After giving a summary of Braverman's thesis Simpkin concludes that '...not only does such an analysis help us to comprehend the way in which we are subject to routine control...it also allows us to begin to understand how the structure of social work has developed since 1970' (Simpkin, 1983, p. 94). He considers that the constraints put in place mean that '...such occupational skills as social workers believed they possessed became diffused and lost' (Simpkin, 1983, p. 94).

In the radical social work paradigm's account of the social work labour process unified, centralised managerial control is, therefore, seen as the dominant experience within manager-social worker relations. This managerial control is considered to have replaced the relatively permissive practice of retrospective supervision (Jones, 1983, p. 124). However, the argument that Social Services Departments introduced new forms of work processes in order to exert greater control over social workers is, for the most part, accompanied by a lack of attention to the details of these changing processes, with the exception of the more detailed consideration given to them by Jones (Jones, 1983, Ch. 7).

Jones identifies two specific forms of control: forms and computers. He argues that official forms in social work are indicative of the changing character of state social work which necessitated closer control over individual social workers (Jones, 1983, p. 123): '...given that the social services are now operationalised within large and complex bureaucracies, they demand social workers who can work in such settings, obey the instructions of managers, and of course fill in the myriad of forms and dossiers which are the life blood of such institutions' (Jones, 1983, p.113). He regards forms not as an inevitable by-product of bureaucratisation but as representing a conscious intervention into the social work labour process (Jones, 1983, p. 124). He argues that the demands of the form can have a significant bearing on contacts between social workers and clients (Jones, 1983, p. 125) and that for the Social Services Department, 'completed forms and records...constitute one of its most crucial sources of information on what is being done by its social workers' (Jones, 1983, p. 123). Forms, from this perspective, are regarded as an old technology put to new use in shaping and monitoring the social work labour process:

> ...the expansion of forms...reflects the long-standing concern to regulate the activities of social workers in their contacts with clients...social services managements have sought to introduce new methods of controlling the interventions of social workers...the growth in the number of forms in Social Services Departments has had a considerable influence in directing such intervention and has been a major factor in the routinisation of social work and the curtailment of professional autonomy. More often than not in contemporary Social Services Departments many of the contacts between social workers and their clients are now to some extent determined by an official form...The demands of the form can have a significant bearing on the nature of the actual contact between the social worker and the client, and if followed, can control at least part of the social worker's actions (Jones, 1983, p. 124).

In concert with the adaptation of the old technology of form filling to the requirements of the changed labour process, the potential of the new technology represented by computers is seen as offering the capacity for further control through the central aggregation of information, increasing the trend towards conception being shifted up the hierarchy and thus establishing further incursions into the social work labour process. Bolger et al. briefly stress the value to managers of information gathered in a form to suit their ends. In particular they highlight '...a direct correspondence within departments with a form of information gathering for the management and the way in which day to day practice is noted and controlled. A department's work can now be summed up in a page of computer print out within a variety of management constructed categories which dominate the thinking and practice of the department' (Bolger et al., 1981. pp. 67-68).

The computerisation of forms and records is considered by Jones to have taken further the detailed process of control over individual pieces of work for two reasons. First, through the curtailment of social workers' penchant for lengthy interpretation of the complexity of problems:

> A most important factor has been the introduction of computerisation of forms and records. That this has led to further restrictions on social worker autonomy arises from the manner in which computerised record keeping prefers information which is expressed very simply, either by a tick or cross against some category, rather than a long interpretive passage from the social worker who tries to capture the complexity of the issues involved (Jones, 1983, p. 125).

Secondly, access is gained to breakdowns of field social workers' workloads: 'A fully integrated computer system has many advantages for a local authority local Social Services Department intent upon securing a disciplined workforce...by a flick of a switch a social work manager can now gain a complete breakdown of an individual social work caseload...' (Jones, 1983, pp. 127-128).   However, Jones acknowledges that the computerisation of Social Services Departments provides 'new possibilities as well as new problems for progressive social workers and clients' (Jones, 1983, p. 130).

Apart from Jones' elaboration of the two examples of control being exerted through forms and computers, passing reference is made by the radical social work writers to the existence of managerial systems and techniques, but they do not indicate in detail what they have in mind (for example operational priority systems, client problem dictionaries, case review, caseload weighting or workload management). The writers are content to give one or two illustrations and the reader is invited to conclude that these illustrations are part and parcel of a general trend towards proletarianisation through greater managerial control of the labour process in social work, a trend they consider to be well advanced. Bolger et al. (1981, p. 67) and Jones (1983, p. 122) align themselves with the proletarianisation thesis, as does Simpkin who concludes that social workers are 'more and more members of a new proletariat...as ever tighter control is exerted over their work process' (Simpkin, 1983, pp. 93-94).

This process of proletarianisation through increasing senior management control is judged to be significant not only because of field social workers' experience of their work being increasingly controlled, but also because of its impact on the social relations of the social work labour process. Simpkin concludes: 'gradually as management attempts to define our jobs more closely, a subordinate hierarchy is being created by a division of labour' (Simpkin, 1983, p. 95). The split between those occupying roles of conception and those charged with execution is regarded as running through the social relations of the social work labour process in Social Services Departments: 'The agency is not a whole; it contains an interiorised division between those working directly with clients and those responsible for management and rationing' (Simpkin, 1983, p. 117). Bolger et al. identify a similar social division in the labour process: 'Some people have to carry out the work of the organisation and others plan it: the two groups are inevitably split and do not have a cross membership. Thus above team leaders there are very few people who ever meet clients; below team leaders there are very few people who structure, plan or co-ordinate...We would underline the increasingly dominant trend in welfare work that separates control and practice further and further' (Bolger et al., 1981, p. 66).

The discussion thus far has identified as a key theme in the radical social work paradigm's representation of the social work labour process that senior management had initiated a process of centralised control over field social workers which influenced significantly the way in which social work is carried out. Managerial techniques which, as we have seen are rarely elaborated but nevertheless presented as a universal trend, are seen as having become *the* forms of control not as possible forms of control. Five points are important in responding to this theme in the radical social work paradigm:

First, the extent to which senior managers were attempting to implement such forms of control is not substantiated by empirical studies.

Secondly, the introduction of managerial techniques can undermine rather than strengthen the control of managers. For example, if a Social Services Department adopts a centralised workload management system, a social worker who is 'up to capacity', in terms of the requisite number of workload points, can use the system as a basis for refusing further work. In other words, management systems the radical social work literature might have regarded as having been set up to control social work can be used by social workers to defend themselves. This point is overlooked in the radical social work literature because of the assumed propensity for managerial techniques always to control workers and extract more labour from them.

Thirdly, in circumstances where managerial techniques have apparently been successfully introduced social workers might apply the techniques in retrospect, rather than allowing their work to be determined by those techniques in advance.

An illuminating comparison here is the way in which police officers interpret the law flexibly - the law becomes a resource rather than a source of straightforward practice. Police studies have shown that police work is structured informally rather than in line with formal requirements and that police personnel use their accepted wisdom to prioritise work and identify objectives (Bittner, 1986). As far as social work is concerned Higgins questions the automatic assumption that there is 'only one type of social worker performing one type of activity' (Higgins, 1980, p. 22) and Pithouse describes the way in which social workers rehearsed accounts of their work for presentation to their supervisors (Pithouse, 1987, Ch. 7), not disclosing those aspects of their work which were incongruent with what was expected (Pithouse, 1987, pp. 76-78). In other words, informal practice may be cloaked in the language of formally acknowledged managerial techniques. The practice of social work supervision is central to this process, combining as it does inspection and consultation in supervisor/supervisee meetings in which the 'good practice' aspects of work are looked at as much as, or usually more than, looking at work from a managerial point of view (Pithouse, 1987, pp. 73-4). The practice of this form of supervision in social work was well-entrenched and the assumption in the radical social work texts that it had been replaced by authoritarian senior management control of social work, needed to be tested rather than asserted.

Fourthly, there is an overriding assumption in the radical social work texts that management can construct inflexible, managerially-determined responses from social workers, that it is in the interests of managers to do so and that it is in social workers' interests to thwart managers. Three points are important here:

- Because of the invisibility of their work, field social workers exercise power over the resource of their own time at the point of contact with service users. Decisions about the amount of time spent and how it is used lie in the social worker's, not the manager's, grasp (Hugman, 1991, p. 125). As Hugman points out, the maintenance of autonomous space in field social work means that its practitioners can bend or break rules in managing requests for assistance in order to accommodate the personal views of the practitioner or the strength of demand from the service user (Hugman, 1991, pp. 72-75);

- Social workers can gain knowledge and skills beyond those of their supervisor and therefore have to be allowed a degree of freedom to undertake their work (Hugman, 1991, p. 64);

- The possibility that social workers might generate their own defensive categorisations in relation to their work is ignored in the radical texts. (See Buckle, 1981, p. 74, for example, on the 'siege mentality' which develops in some intake teams).

Fifthly, the radical social work accounts of the introduction of managerial techniques rest on an implicit belief in a golden age in which social workers were autonomous, creative, therapeutic agents: '...the social worker must enjoy a degree of autonomy and discretion in the relationship...Consequently the social worker needs to be trusted in practice, as it is deemed undesirable for the interaction between social worker and client to be regulated closely and directly by the employing authority, for to do so would jeopardise the therapeutic relationship' (Jones, 1983, p. 78). It is only possible to hold on to this implicit belief in a disappearing golden age of therapeutic relationships if the core of long-standing statutory duties at the centre of social work, which were inherited rather than initiated in the post-Seebohm era, are ignored.   (See Handler [1968] for a pre-Seebohm example of controlling and coercive practice by Child Care Officers in relation to social work with 'problem families'). In the radical social work texts the implicit belief in a golden age clouds the issue of exactly what managerial control of social work in the post-Seebohm period is being measured against. The lament for some ideal state of social work once having existed is surely dubious: 'Changes mean that social workers now have to spend most of their time trying to juggle with the impossible demands of a large caseload...The actual texture of contemporary social work practice in most local authorities is rapidly moving away from the professional ideals of the activity' (Jones, 1983, pp. 112-113). Again, if a pre-Seebohm comparison is made with Handler's study of the work of Child Care Officers it is difficult to locate the professional ideals of social work in many of their activities, such as household budgeting and collecting rent, despite radical social work writers' depiction of those ideals as having existed.

This section has considered a key theme in the radical social work paradigm: senior management's centralised control of the social work labour process. However, as we saw in Chapter Two the labour process perspective identified not only the existence of control strategies but also the continual problem which exists in transforming labour power into actual labour power because of worker resistance. It is to the radical social work paradigm's treatment of this theme that the next section now turns.

The indeterminacy of labour power: is labour readily susceptible to managerial domination?

Alongside the heavy emphasis on senior management control, developed around the separation of conception and execution, the radical social work paradigm's approach to the social work labour process allows for the indeterminacy of labour power which was considered in the review of the post-Braverman debate in Chapter Two. Radical social work writers acknowledge the problem of transforming labour power into actual labour on three fronts: at the levels of individual practice, the team unit and the trade union.

Simpkin implies that, despite the crushing managerial control he identifies, there is still some room in which social workers can manoeuvre: '...fundamental to any radical approach must be a challenge to the artificial divisions which are made between social workers and clients...The essence of radicalism is...to recognise that to a large extent our fate is shared' (Simpkin, 1983, p. 2). Jones' articulation of the room for manoeuvre at the level of individual practice is more explicit. He contends that the extent to which social work operates either in the interests of the state or in the interests of service users depends largely on social workers themselves, because as a form of state intervention social work is distinguished by its highly intensive and personalised approach. The emphases within social work on building relationships and the ability of the social worker to effect change mean that the social worker must enjoy a degree of autonomy and discretion and, as a consequence, the social worker has to be trusted at the level of direct practice, rather than being closely and directly regulated by the employing authority (Jones, 1983, p. 78). Jones claims that even what he describes as the most traditional and conservative of caseworkers sometimes work in ways which are contrary to the state's interests (Jones, 1983, p. 78). He fleshes out the argument that there is room for manoeuvre with the following examples of low-level strategies of professional deviance: social workers who ignore service users' manipulation of the social security system; 'being less rigorous than many social work managers would like in the use of material aid...and preparing social enquiry reports in juvenile court proceedings which protect some youngsters from the more punitive aspects of the legal system' (Jones, 1983, p. 80).

Bolger et al. adopt a similar position in arguing that the practice of casework allows social workers to maintain areas of work shielded from direct management intervention which belong 'almost exclusively to the social worker and client' (Bolger et al., 1981. p. 99). They suggest that management control can only be achieved in this area by indirect means such as supervision and that this space can be occupied by the 'professional saboteurs' and 'middle class bandits' depicted by Pearson (Pearson, 1973; 1975). Although Bolger et al. consider this space to be under attack from computerised records and de-skilling, the space is nevertheless seen as allowing a different form of direct interaction with service users to occur:

> This is one clear reason why Social Services Department welfare workers can be seen as the direct allies of working people as against the way in which the rent collector and the social security clerk are experienced by working people....The very privacy of that relationship allows the social worker to practice outside dominant state ideologies...The very privatised nature of the social work interview means that the courses of action are not laid down in detail (Bolger et al., 1981, p. 101).

With the benefit of hindsight, one of the striking characteristics of the radical social work discussion of practice is the way in which the issue of autonomy in work with service users is considered solely in relation to establishing some space free from management control, with the consequent exclusion of the question of social workers' accountability to service users.

Teamwork

Moving beyond the level of individual practice, in the radical social work texts the social services organisation is seen as a 'target for practice' (Corrigan and Leonard, 1978, p. 155). In stressing the indeterminacy of labour power within the organisation, two interlocking strategies of worker resistance are advocated as counter measures to managerial control strategies: developing teamwork on a more collective basis and building workplace trade unionism. 'Material experiences with trade unionism and in collective work' are considered to be at the heart of worker resistance (Bolger et al., 1981, p. 81).

In part the emphasis on teamwork in radical social work texts is simply a plea for reducing the importance of status differentials in day-to-day working relationships. In this egalitarian vein, Bailey and Brake emphasise the need for teams to develop 'collective, de-hierarchised practice' (Bailey and Brake, 1980, p. 19) and Bennett repudiates the view that someone's place in the local team's hierarchy should define 'speaking rights' (Bennett, 1980, p. 160). However, the aspirations for what could be achieved through teamwork are not limited to the promotion of more egalitarian working relationships. They are also considered as a component in a wider political programme: '...an essential principle of moving towards socialist practice is that welfare workers must work within a collective framework' (Bolger et al., 1981, p. 62), as a counterweight to the 'individuation process' (Bolger et al., 1981, p. 81). Bolger et al. argue that the establishment of decentralised teams in Social Services Departments carried with it the 'possibility of providing a counterweight to balance the increased bureaucracy...It provides the possibility of a collective team practice and experience' which works against 'an individualised, de-skilled hierarchical experience (Bolger et al., 1981, pp. 67-68). In other words, teamwork is a form of resistance to managerial control of the social work labour process. Teamwork stands in 'contradiction to the centralised bureaucratic power not only in the Social Services Department, but in the corporate management structure of the whole local authority' (Bolger et al., 1981, p. 61).

As part of a proposed radical programme for social work, the development of collective teamwork is presented by Corrigan and Leonard as a core component of the class struggle in which social workers are considered to be engaged (Corrigan and Leonard, 1978, pp. 115-7). Simpkin goes further in claiming that:

> One major goal of radical social work has been to foster teamwork, not just for its own sake or for the maintenance and improvement of standards which will

result, but for its political consequences. A team which functions co-operatively is a break in the hierarchical command. The political conclusions which will be forced on any such team will lead it to extend solidarity towards other workers and towards clients. Two consequences are likely to occur. Firstly, the working lives of team members will be enhanced if they are able to assert greater control over their jobs...Secondly, the collective security engendered is likely to make social work a much more open affair, which will in turn allow clients a greater freedom in and choice over what help they get' (Simpkin, 1983, p.178).

Workplace trade unionism

Having stressed some room for manoeuvre at the level of individual practice and the need to develop collective teamwork to counter the encroachment of managerial control strategies, radical social work writers also emphasise the 'countervailing tendency of increased trade union activity' (Bolger et al., 1981, p. 67) as 'an alternative structure to that of management' (Garrett, 1980, pp. 210-211). The arguments employed to explore and advocate workplace trade unionism are similar to those developed in relation to the desirability of teamwork.

For Bolger et al. trade union activity creates a set of social relationships which are moving towards a collectivism generated by a reaction against the individualisation and atomisation of the experience of work (Bolger et al., 1981, p. 64):

> A centralised form and structure of welfare work has constructed a de-skilled and individualised work force. This experience...stripped away the veils of ideology around such things as "professional autonomy". It increased welfare workers' perception of themselves as workers...We are stressing the objective process of proletarianisation which turns people into pure members of the labour force and we are suggesting that this process has increased in magnitude over the recent period....We are suggesting that this set of experiences has a direct impact upon workers' consciousness...This experience then begins to mirror increasingly the normal experience of labour in a capitalist society. That experience on a day-to-day basis constructs a different form of collectivity around the trade union movement; around forms of experience and struggle which overcome that atomised experience. It is this collectivity which is the bedrock experience of trade unionism and which social workers began to express...What constructs trade union consciousness and activity is the move towards collective experience and activity in a work environment that is essentially individualising (Bolger et al., 1981, p. 71).

Simpkin has similar recourse to an industrial comparison in his analysis of the development of collectivist social work trade unionism:

The new conditions began to impose some solidarity among people who were traditionally individualists. We began to stand together both in support of client needs and to better our own conditions. Just as by 1915 unionisation had forced its way into Fords, so social workers...began to develop a trade union consciousness informed by our own plight and that of our clients...The widespread acceptance of trade union values sprang from the conditions and needs we all shared (Simpkin, 1983, p. 19).

This impetus towards trade union collectivism as a counterweight to management control is seen as developing out of a movement away from professional consciousness as the labour process is restructured under the control of management (Bolger et al., 1981, p. 65; Jones, 1983, p. 132): 'The joining of a trade union should not be taken simply as reflecting a move towards a more radical politics...The growth of trade union membership...is a reflection of the changing nature of the state's personal social services. The reduction in professional autonomy and the increasing tendency for local authorities to regard their social workers primarily as employees have not been conducive to the promotion of a professional consciousness' (Jones, 1983, pp. 132-134). Bolger et al. develop the point that social workers are only employees in arguing that social workers have only their labour power to sell and are therefore members of the working class. Trade unionism is located in the context of this class position: 'Relations between welfare workers, manual industrial workers and welfare clients are relations within a class and not between classes' (Bolger et al., 1981, p. 22). For Jones workplace trade unionism is not just a defensive reaction against professional consciousness and a product of social workers' class location. It is a forward-moving force for transforming the labour process: 'The development and extension of trade unionism amongst social workers...is opening up new possibilities for social workers who are intent upon both defending social work clients from further attacks and transforming the nature of welfare generally' (Jones, 1983, p. 6).
In each of these accounts, workplace trade unionism is presented as field social workers' response to objective changes in the social work labour process: 'The recent experience of working within local authorities has compelled many social workers to think of themselves more as wage labour than professionals, and it is this development which has been a crucial influence in the growth of trade unionism' (Jones, 1983, p. 134). Field social workers, it is argued, are increasingly conscious of their position as workers. Simpkin makes the point in relation to the field social workers' strike of 1978-9, locating its origins as much in field social workers' experience of their work as in a financial imperative: 'The strikes were not simply about money but were an expression of the rising tide of disillusion and resentment of the demands made on social workers and the structures in which they were expected to operate' (Simpkin, 1983, p.152).
For radical social work writers then, workplace trade unionism is evidence of social workers' resistance to managerial control strategies. Trade union activity is

seen as social workers' response to a labour process in which they find themselves increasingly alienated. But the trade union is also seen as having an important role in defending field social workers' interests in relation to 'day-to-day work organisation as well as salaries and general conditions of service because the trade unions offer the best means for securing better wages and improved working conditions' (Jones, 1983, p. 135) and negotiating conditions governing the introduction of new working practices (Simpkin, 1983, p. 144). As Simpkin states, social workers joined a trade union to pursue their own interests: 'Nearly all social workers now accept the need for some collective association to protect their interests and secure more favourable pay and conditions...essentially we join the union to pursue our own interests, and social workers are at last abandoning earnest self-sacrifice in pursuit of better pay and holidays as well as working conditions which can improve the response to clients' needs' (Simpkin, 1983, pp. 144-145).

To any trade unionist, none of the claims about the defensive and betterment potential of trade union membership would be surprising. However, radical writers (see for example, Bailey and Brake, 1980, pp. 19-20), go further and argue that field social workers can also use a trade union to defend service users' interests: '...all social workers must join and play a part in their union, because it is only by doing this that they will be able to utilise the union to defend both themselves and their clients' interests' (Corrigan and Leonard, 1978, pp. 143-144). Simpkin views trade unionism as the bridge across the social worker-service user boundary, a demonstration of class solidarity: 'joining a union should not be a purely self-interested act but a recognition of a direct link, a shared fate with all those who are exploited by the owners or controllers of capital' (Simpkin, 1983, p. 157).

The claims for both teamwork and trade unionism represent far-reaching goals not just for social workers but through them also for service users. From this distance, it is interesting to note the confidence with which radical social work writers see social workers as capable of safeguarding and extending service users' interests. Service users' interests and social workers' interests are seen as coalescing in the political practice of teamwork and trade unionism activism.

As we saw in Chapter Two, the post-Braverman debate within the labour process perspective focused not only on the indeterminacy of labour power, and the possibilities within that indeterminacy for worker resistance, but also countenanced the possibility of worker consent, which is discussed in the next section.

Worker consent: does labour always have to be actively controlled by management?

In the previous section, a central theme which emerged in the radical social work paradigm's representation of the social work labour process was the essential unity of field social workers' interests in developing collective oppositional strategies, through teamwork and trade union activism, which exploited the indeterminacy of labour power. In adopting this stance the potential for worker consent is obscured in the radical social work texts. When radical social work writers give a glimpse of divisions amongst field social workers they are quickly spirited away. Unity of oppositional interests is presented as the material reality, division and the possibility of worker consent are seen as a petty distraction:

> It is vital to attempt to work collectively with colleagues and to keep them informed. At some time or other, we all tend to think that the people we work with are fools, reactionaries, old-fashioned, careerists, boring, wet radicals and just plain lunatics; there are times when they are exasperating because they will not listen. Such feelings on some occasions are inevitable, but they are completely counter-productive (Corrigan and Leonard, 1978, p. 155).

In contrast, Salaman argues that the development amongst workers of 'full-blown consciousness of interests...is rare...Even when worker relations are so patterned as to give rise to the distinctive structures of solidarity in opposition...it is clear that this is only rarely related to the experience of shared interests and the determination to act to advance them' (Salaman, 1986, p. 91).

Given the lack of empirical evidence concerning stances adopted by social workers in the labour process, nothing else can be added to this note on the absence of the possibility of worker consent in the radical social work texts to suggest consent as a possible alternative to the oppositional stance which, within the radical social work paradigm, is assumed to be widespread.

Monolithic management: is management a unified coherent interest?

'Management' is presented in the radical social work texts as a powerful, monolithic interest. The possibility that there might be divisions within management (Crompton and Jones, 1984, p. 96) with diverse interests is not recognised. For example, it may be that there are differences of interest between those managers with responsibility for policy and resource allocation and those managers who are charged with trying to ensure field social workers carry out policy and who vet applications for departmental resources. Again, the point to be made is that representations of management as a monolithic interest have not been tested empirically.

Radical social work writers' depiction of management as monolithic leads to their neglect both of the wider political context of the location of the personal social services in local authorities and of the internal workings of Social Services Departments, particularly in so far as the relationships between managers and social workers outside trade union/management negotiations are concerned. Only a very limited view of senior managers is presented in the radical social work texts. This view ignores the key position in the social work labour process occupied by front-line managers who are usually outside formal trade union and management negotiations. Therefore the radical texts' emphasis on trade union activism and industrial relations issues throws little light on the way in which the management of field social work is actually undertaken. In other words, a missing dimension in the radical social work texts is the *process* of organisational structure in day-to-day work. For example, if managerial control is being exerted exactly how is that impacting on the work of field social workers supervised by front-line managers?

In the radical social work texts' representation of the social work labour process there is little discussion about the position and functions of front-line managers, in relation to the identified developments towards managerial control. The emphasis on collective teamwork sketches out a scenario in which the interests of a social work team as a whole are set against the interests of senior managers. There appears to be a tacit assumption that the front-line manager will be swept along on the wave of team collectivity and that her/his interests lie with those of her/his team. The cut-off point in terms of the definition of shared interests is only rarely identified:

> Thus the agency is not a whole. It contains an interiorised division between those working directly with clients and those responsible for management and rationing which no form of representation and mutual discussion can solve. There is no more unenviable post than that of area officer, who is supposed to embody both functions at once; it is not surprising that most opt for the easier life in supporting management. We are not all engaged in the same task, as the managerial myth would have it, and our relationships must proceed in recognition of the fact. I do not advocate destructive hostility; we do need a modus vivendi...but they now represent a different interest and are isolated from the main body of workers (Simpkin, 1983, p. 117).

This quotation is interesting not just for its depiction of how interests are divided and defined but also for the way in which the day-to-day negotiation of the social work labour process, 'a modus vivendi', is dismissed as a consciously, and perhaps cynically, erected surface veneer rather than being taken seriously as an object of study. Bolger et al. echo Simpkin's basic division of interest between managers and workers, also using a division of labour based on client contact as a means of articulating the separation of conception and execution, and in the process, like Simpkin, they bracket front-line managers in with social workers: 'Some people have to carry out the work of the organisation and others have to plan it: the two groups are inevitably split and do not have a cross membership. Thus, above team leaders there are very few people who ever meet clients; below team leaders there are very few people who are structurally allowed to plan or co-ordinate' (Bolger et al., 1981, p. 66).

The drift of all this is clear. There is a dividing line above front-line manager level across which the interests of field social workers and middle and senior managers diverge. The interests of fieldworkers lie one way and the interests of managers the other. However, in the radical social work literature the impact on front-line managers of this divergence of interests is not placed in an empirical context with one exception, a brief discussion by Bennett of his experiences as a front-line manager. Bennett provides some tantalising glimpses into how the representation of the social work labour process in radical texts might obscure the tensions which operated day-to-day in the social work labour process. Bennett's account is of a 'team approach to neighbourhood field work practice' (Bennett, 1980, p. 155). Bennett states that in West Kensington the team was operating on a more collective basis but that he, as the team leader, still had an 'executive function' (Bennett, 1980, p. 161) and 'day-to-day accountability for workers' performance' (Bennett, 1980, p. 180). He notes that 'it has always been assumed that the managerial, supervisory and accountability aspects would be kept within the departmental norm...Day-to-day management of the office was therefore to be undertaken by the team leader, who in turn was to maintain close links with the area officer' (Bennett, 1980, p. 158). From Bennett's own account of his experience of front-line management, he appeared to be at the centre of tensions between greater collectivity in the local team and traditional patterns of managerial accountability. We learn little from his account about how this tension was played out. For example, the level of collective responsibility within the team was to be 'appropriate' (Bennett, 1980, p. 177) and Bennett 'had to learn to combine management accountability with my contribution to the collective approach' (Bennett, 1980, p. 180). We are not told how this combination was effected other than it 'required a high level of integrity by all team members' (Bennett, 1980, p. 180).

Pithouse's study of a Welsh Social Services Department illuminates something of the nature of the tension which is only alluded to by Bennett. He argues that practice and management are brought together in the role of front-line manager and that the supervisory role of the first line of management is crucial. In contrast to the monolithic management interest depicted in the radical social work texts, Pithouse found that those front-line managers who were regarded as 'good' supervisors by social workers were those who 'demonstrate to their teams their *independence from higher management* and their *disinclination to intrude overtly* in the workers day-to-day practices' (my emphasis, Pithouse, 1987, p. 65).

Conclusion

The common position of the radical social work texts, as we have seen, is that in the post-Seebohm period managerial control strategies eroded the autonomy of field social workers. Radical social work writers identify the potential for resistance to managerial control strategies, arguing that some room for manoeuvre still existed at the level of individual practice and that the dual workplace-based strategies of trade unionism activism and collective teamwork could be used to combat the encroachment of managerial control. In the course of this Chapter's review of the radical social work paradigm's representation of the imposition of an industrial model of managerial control on the social work labour process, questions have been raised in relation to four issues: first, the extent to which managerial techniques of control were introduced; secondly, the exclusive emphasis on collective oppositional strategies; thirdly the neglect of worker consent; fourthly, the assumption of the existence of a monolithic management interest and the consequent neglect of the position of front-line managers.

In summary, the accumulated weight of questions in relation to these four issues suggests that the radical social work paradigm's use of Braverman's thesis as a model for the social work labour process leads to its failure to explore social work's distinctiveness. The neglect of the distinctiveness of the social work labour process is the product of the radical social work texts' adoption of a structuralist stance in their analysis of the labour process. Following Braverman, who suggested his analysis could be extended from industry to many white collar occupations (Braverman, 1974, p. 408), radical social work writers assume that pervasive managerial control is a universal process across occupations. As a consequence, radical writers are concerned with outlining broad and general features of developments in the structure of the social work labour process, in line with the early concerns of the post-Braverman debate (Thompson and McHugh, 1990, pp. 20-23). They are concerned with the playing out in a specific context of broad tendencies in the world of work, rather than with variations in the particular work setting of social work. Adopting this orthodox Bravermanian approach leads radical social work writers to an understanding of participation in the social work labour process in terms of broad sectional interests. Individual actors in the social work labour process, whether managers or field social workers, are seen only as personifications of general structural processes, as simply bearers of a mode of production.

In stressing the excessively structuralist stance taken within the radical social work paradigm, it is, of course, important to hold on to the location of the social work labour process in an organisational structure. However, in order to understand the operation of the social work labour process it has to be studied as both a structure and a process. In other words, the social work labour process cannot be simply and unambiguously read off from its organisational structure. As Hugman points out work structures have a matter-of-fact place in the perceptions of people working within them and hierarchical power is exercised through routinised sets of expectations about objectives, methods and so on (Hugman, 1991, p. 66). The radical social work texts' emphasis on broad, antagonistic sectional interests emphasised differences in structural location and in so doing obscured possible similarities in routinised expectations across different structural locations in the social work labour process.

What this concluding discussion suggests is the need to understand not just the organisational structure of the labour process but also how individuals operate within it. It points to the interdependence of structure and process. For example, in relation to front-line management it is important to know the position occupied by front-line managers in the organisational structure of the social work labour process but it is also important to know how the occupants of those 'slots' in the organisational structure of the labour process interpret their position in day-to-day work processes. Such a consideration of the social work labour process did not surface in the radical social work paradigm. The paradigm remained rooted in an analysis based on commodity production for surplus value, arguing that the management processes associated with private sector production were transferred into social work. The discussion thus far seems to cast doubt on whether the organisational structures and processes associated with the provision of state social work can be understood through a model geared to explaining capitalist production (Thompson and McHugh, 1990, p. 42). Ramsay et al. argue that detailed study of the nature and direction of specific labour processes in the public sector is needed (Ramsay et al., 1991, p. 38). In contrast, the radical social work writers seemed not to have faced up to the implications of analysing the specific labour process of an occupation which, they concluded, retained at the least a degree of autonomy over the carrying out of its work. Accordingly, in the next chapter an attempt is made to develop the basis for an alternative model of the social work labour process to that of the industrial model of the radical social work paradigm.

4 Social work as a bureau-professional state labour process

Introduction

Chapter Three's review of the representation of the social work labour process in the radical social work texts demonstrated that radical social work writers were working largely within the limitations of an orthodox Bravermanian labour process perspective, augmented by some attention to the indeterminacy of labour power, an indeterminacy which they regarded as being eroded at the level of individual practice, as social work came under increasing managerial control. In so doing, the radical social work literature in some cases neglected and in some cases predated the growing sophistication of the labour process perspective which occurred in the post-Braverman debate, as outlined in Chapter Two.

In Chapter Two, the loosening up of the labour process perspective was presented as having identified problems in the application of an orthodox Bravermanian model to workers in surplus value producing sectors. However, the extent to which the labour process perspective could be used to explain developments in the organisation of work in the state sector, where surplus value production was not the objective and where the political and ideological context was therefore significant, was not explored by the post-Braverman literature reviewed in Chapter Two. Braverman himself made no distinction between workers in the surplus value producing sectors and those in the state sector. By implication, and as we saw in Chapter Three the radical social work writers followed him in this, Braverman assumed that the process of encroaching managerial control he identified was universally applicable.

The discussion of the legacy of Marx at the beginning of Chapter Two highlighted the distinction between a general labour process concerned with the production of use values and a specifically capitalist labour process concerned with generating surplus value, with the implication being that all forms of work can not be understood through a labour process perspective geared to explaining capitalist production (Thompson and McHugh, 1990, p. 42). The central concern of this chapter is to draw on a range of work which allows consideration to be given to the basis from which the labour process perspective needs to be developed in order to take account of the distinctive features of the social work labour process as state welfare work Accordingly, the chapter begins by locating the social work labour process within the state, then explores the distinctiveness of state-mediated professional work, before giving an account of the consolidation of the bureau-professional structure of the social work labour process in the context of the social democratic welfare state. In that account, the significance of decentralised Area Teams, within the bureau-professional structure of Social Services Departments, emerges.

State labour processes

As we saw in Chapter Two, in the post-Braverman debate the determinism of Braverman's model was questioned and an expanded   framework was developed within which to explore the operational intricacies of the labour process. That framework has to be expanded still further by moving the labour process perspective some distance from its roots in the analysis of capitalist manufacturing industry and into an analysis of social work. The importance of making such a move is supported by critiques of the labour process perspective. Such critiques have argued that both the production process, and its specifically capitalist basis in valorisation, have been elbowed aside in the heavy attention given by the labour process perspective to managerial control (Cohen, 1987; Morgan and Hooper, 1987; Storey, 1985).   Morgan and Hooper contend that the obscuring of the specifically capitalist underpinnings of supposedly generic approaches to the study of the labour process resulted in the widespread assumption that 'location within a set of capitalist relations, as opposed to working within the state, makes little difference' (Morgan and Hooper, 1987, p. 609). On the contrary, Morgan and Hooper argue that the extent to which particular activities are linked to the market or are insulated from the market is crucial and that 'there has been little discussion of these macro-level determinants of managerial strategies...particularly as far as the state sector is concerned' (Morgan and Hopper, 1987, p. 624). Similarly, Smith et al recognise the difficulties in translating a theory concerned with the extraction of surplus value for private accumulation into the public sector (Smith et al, 1991, p. 2). Thompson and McHugh suggest that the state service sector generates different employment relations (Thompson and McHugh, 1990, p. 116) and that not all forms of work can be understood through a labour process perspective geared to explaining capitalist production (Thompson and McHugh, 1990, p. 42): 'The whole process of [public service] management is a complex bargaining and balancing act. While this may be true of all management, the factors which shape it in public services are both distinctive and more wide ranging' (Thompson and McHugh, 1990, p. 128). In the light of these criticisms of the labour process perspective, taking forward a distinctive model of the social work labour process, through its location in the state, appears to be justified and in line with a more general recognition of the importance of the state being more than a 'shadowy background factor' in the labour process perspective (Thompson and McHugh, 1990, p. 11).

Marx's distinction between a general labour process for the production of use values and the specifically capitalist labour process concerned with the production of surplus value is a helpful starting point. In the analysis of state welfare work, the political context of the state's production of use values replaces the economic context of the market's generation of surplus value. In Neo-Marxist theories of the state, the distinctiveness of state labour processes is seen as lying in their political location and their being subject to political contingencies. Habermas (1976), O'Connor (1973) and Offe (1983) highlight the fact that the state negates capitalist social relations as well as reproducing them. As a result, policy-making is subject to diffuse pressures and its implementation is characterised by the existence of diverse objectives (Cousins, 1987, p. 4). It is the presence of diffuse pressures and diverse objectives within the state which leads Neo-Marxist writers to stress that the state's role as employer of labour, stressed in more orthodox economistic Marxist accounts, is only one of the state's roles. Offe, for example, argues that different areas of state employment are organised in different modes from the bureaucratic mode involved in allocative state activities such as making social security payments, through to a democratic mode involving political conflict and consensus. He also maintains that whilst the state has to be organised in ways which will meet the pressures to sustain the accumulation process, it nevertheless depends on the compliance of professional labour in those state occupations which have retained some autonomy on the basis of expertise (Offe, 1975).

Neo-Marxist analyses are then useful as a starting point for contextualising the present discussion. They emphasise the importance of the state as the political domain in which certain labour processes are located. However, macro-level accounts of the distinctiveness of state location have to be fleshed out further in order to take forward the basis for a model of the social work labour process. Offe's emphasis on the significance of professional labour within the state is particularly pertinent and is taken as the starting point for the next section.

Professional work and the state

Johnson's discussion of professional work (Johnson, 1972) is an attempt to move beyond trait approaches (Greenwood, 1957; Carr-Saunders and Wilson, 1962; Etzioni, 1969; Toren, 1972). As an alternative to the preoccupation with the extent to which various occupations have taken on the mantle of a 'true' profession,

Johnson analyses professions as structures of power within occupations. He identifies three types of professional power structures: collegiate, for example medicine; patronage, for example architecture; and mediated, for example social work. In the case of mediated professions an agency, usually a state organisation, acts as mediator between the profession and its clientele in deciding   who the profession's clientele will be and in broad terms what should be provided for that clientele through a legal framework and the overall allocation of resources. The state acts as the corporate patron of agencies which provide services on its behalf (Johnson, 1972, p. 77).

Johnson's analysis of the power structures in which professional work is located is helpful in carrying forward an attempt to reformulate the social work labour process. Much of the writing on professional work (for example, Wilding, 1982) stresses the centrality and similarity of power across professions in relation to professional workers' clientele. Such work is clearly focusing on important issues concerning the power wielded by professionals in relation to the recipients of their services but for our present purpose, Johnson moves on consideration of the social work labour process from the question posed by the traits school (is a particular occupation a profession?) to a focus on how a particular occupation has been professionalised within a range of possible organisational arrangements for the structuring of its work.   However, Johnson's work also has limitations in terms of its usefulness as a basis for reformulating the social work labour process. Whilst he marks out the distinctiveness of mediated professional work, as one organisational variant, he does not move on to an analysis of the organisational structures in which such mediated professional work is located nor to how those structures have shaped professional work. These concerns are addressed by Derber (1982; 1983) through an analysis which clarifies how the labour process perspective needs to be modified to encompass the distinctiveness of professional work within the state, as identified by Johnson.

Derber begins his analysis by highlighting the extent to which professional work has become salaried employment rather than being conducted on an independent basis. He argues that widespread dependent employment of this type has implications for the organisation of professional work and the identity of the professional worker (Derber, 1983, p. 309). This is in contrast to the orthodox Bravermanian approach which, we saw in Chapter Two, maintained that the wresting of control over professional work is a similar process to that experienced by manual workers. Derber locates the origin of the orthodox Bravermanian approach in an elision between the existence of salaried contractual employment and the subordination of professional work, based on management's appropriation of power over the labour process (Derber, 1983, p. 311). The orthodox Bravermanian perspective suggested that 'Lacking the resources to maintain an independent economic position, professionals are absorbed within large-scale organisational corporate and state bureaucracies and become subject like other employees to heteronomous management, authority and control and to degradation of status and reward' (Derber, 1983, p. 310).

In contrast to this orthodox Bravermanian position, Derber argues for the distinctiveness of the labour processes of professional workers which, he maintains, do not follow the industrial model. In order to demonstrate the distinctiveness of professional labour processes, Derber poses a central question: what does lack of control over work mean? As we saw in Chapter Two, Braverman follows Marx in suggesting that it has two components: lack of control over the process of labour and lack of control over the uses of the product. The first component highlights the tendency for the purchasers of labour power to impose their own conception of how to organise and execute the job. The second component points to the purchasers' control over what is produced and the purpose for which it is used, and, in commercial operations, how and when it is sold (Derber, 1983, p. 312). In other words, Derber argues, the first component is about the *means* and the second component about the *ends* of the labour process (Derber, 1983, p. 313). As we saw in Chapters Two and Three the labour process perspective developed around issues which addressed the first component, the means of the labour process and managerial control over it. Derber argues that the emphasis in the labour process perspective on this first component - lack of control over the process of work - came to be synonymous with proletarianisation itself (Derber, 1983, p. 315). As a result, the second component - lack of control over the ends of work - was ignored. Derber refers to this second component as 'ideological proletarianisation', the management control exerted over the goals and purposes of work and the workers' powerlessness to define the final product of work and the use to which it is put. As Derber emphasises, most industrial workers experience both the technical and ideological components of control simultaneously and this has allowed the labour process perspective to concentrate its attentions on the former (Derber, 1983, p. 313).

Having disaggregated technical and ideological proletarianisation, Derber suggests that in the case of professional work: 'Ideological proletarianisation creates a type of worker whose integrity is threatened less by the expropriation of his (sic) skill than his values or sense of purpose. It reduces the domain of freedom and creativity to problems of technique...It is the lack of control over the ends to which work is put that, in the current period, defines most centrally their (professionals') proletarianisation' (Derber, 1983, p. 316). Derber concedes that, with the move to salaried employment, professionals might have had their responsibilities narrowed and their range of tasks constricted but even if this is the case, he emphasises that these responsibilities and tasks still demand the most skill and discretion (Derber, 1983, pp. 317-318). Thus professional workers maintain a considerable degree of technical autonomy.

Derber suggests that professional workers can adapt to ideological proletarianisation through ideological co-optation, a process of redefining the goals of their work so that the disparities between professional and organisational interests are minimised and their employing organisations are perceived as committed to professional workers' underlying values and purposes: 'Ideological co-optation reflects the new hybrid identity in which professionals take their moral values and objectives from their new institutional employers, but sustain an identity separate from other employees by their investment in technical expertise' (Derber, 1983, p. 330-331). Derber's analysis is pitched at the level of trying to identify general trends in the labour processes of professional work, but it is sprinkled with illustrations of the sort of developments he has in mind. As far as social work is concerned he argues that 'The therapeutic approach formed the basis for a highly sophisticated ideological co-optation, where social workers' moral concerns for the well-being of their clients could be accommodated in a form of practice that served institutional ends' (Derber, 1983, p. 333). The final point in Derber's analysis, which relates to the concerns of this chapter in reformulating the social work labour process, is that the continued possession of technical knowledge and skill by professional workers may serve management's interests more than it threatens them and there is then no imperative for technical proletarianisation (Derber, 1983, p. 335).

Derber's distinction between ideological and technical proletarianisation is useful. It suggests that some state welfare professionals may retain considerable degrees of technical autonomy in determining responses to service users' needs. The labour process of such workers cannot be seen as automatically subject to the loss of control over work which an orthodox Bravermanian approach and the radical social work writers see as the central development. Derber's thesis suggests the need for more detailed work to be undertaken on opening up the operation of particular labour processes (see the next section) an approach which Witz regards as essential if occupations are to escape from being seen as merely 'specimens of a more general fixed concept' (Witz, 1990, p. 675).

Before considering the social work labour process itself in more detail, it should be noted that Derber's work is consistent with Jamous and Peloille's analysis (Jamous and Peloille, 1970) which also suggests why social work may not be as susceptible to technical proletarianisation as the radical social work writers claim. Jamous and Peloille distinguish between the 'technicality' and 'indetermination' components of professional knowledge. Technicality is the extent which a systematic body of knowledge is used in the justification of occupational expertise. Indeterminacy refers to aspects of uncertainty in occupational knowledge which are the basis of an occupation's mystique or the source of its legitimation, for instance non-transferable or esoteric skills. Jamous and Peloille claim that professions are occupations which have a high indeterminacy/technicality ratio. Those professions that successfully project a high degree of indeterminacy will be less susceptible to managerial or bureaucratic intervention and can claim a measure of work autonomy. Thus, whilst social work may be criticised from some quarters on the grounds of its indeterminacy, it may be precisely its possession of this quality which makes it difficult to control: 'Professional insulation from external controls is likely to be greatest where the outcomes of professional activities are relatively vague and intangible...This may be a factor in professional attachment to psychotherapeutic casework' (Sibeon, 1991, p. 27). This claim to the indeterminacy of social work may facilitate its insulation from technical control. (It may also be the basis on which social workers and front-line managers negotiate their 'parochial professionalism' [see Chapter Eight]).

Thus, the concept of indeterminacy in the work of Jamous and Peloille and the distinction between ideological and technical control in the work of Derber alerts us first, to the possibility of social work presenting some difficulty in terms of the achievement of managerial control over the social work labour process and secondly, to the question of whether this is even a necessary or desirable goal for management.   Having introduced the distinctive nature of professional labour processes, through the work of Johnson, Derber, and Jamous and Peloille, the next section contextualises this distinctiveness as far as social work is concerned in its specific state location.

The social work labour process in the welfare state

Cawson's (1982) approach to state/professional relations represents professional workers as engaged in negotiations with the state.   On one side of these negotiations professionals provide expertise in exchange for favourable policies and resources. On the other side, the state needs professionals to supply services and legitimate state intervention in terms of their expertise. The particular nature of the professional/state relations settlement in the case of social work will now be considered.

In drawing on Johnson (to locate social work as a mediated occupation within the state), Derber, Jamous and Peloille (to highlight distinctive aspects of professional labour processes), and Cawson (to emphasise state/professional relations) it is important to avoid slipping back into ideal types of professionalisation. To do so would suggest that social workers had the opportunity to develop professional autonomy, separate from the state, and that at a later stage the state interposed itself between social work and its clientele. No such sequential approach can be taken to the study of the social work labour process. It can only be approached through stressing first, its embeddedness in social democratic ideology and secondly, the manifestation of this ideology in the bureau-professional organisational form promoted by the Seebohm Report (Seebohm, 1968). Such an approach is necessary because the labour process perspective has insufficiently explored the consequences of social work's location in the welfare state. Mishra argues that it is impossible to examine welfare state organisations and the professions in isolation from each other (Mishra, 1984, p. 177). It is to the social democratic context in which social work was located, and the bureau-professional form of the labour process this engendered, that the discussion now turns.

The Seebohm Report: consolidating the social work labour process in a social democratic ideological context

The post-war social democratic consensus has been described as the 'set of commitments, assumptions and expectations, transcending party conflicts and shared by the great majority of the country's political and economic leaders which provided the framework within which policy decisions were made' (Marquand, 1988, p. 18). The consensus supported the welfare state as the 'totality of schemes and services through which central government together with the local authorities assumed a major responsibility for dealing with all the different types of social problems which beset individual citizens' (Marwick, 1990, p. 45). The consolidation of social work's position, from being a relatively marginal collection of roles and practices to a central and systematically organised element of welfare in the social democratic welfare state (Clarke, 1979, p. 127), was achieved through the production of the Seebohm Report and its implementation.

The origins of the Seebohm Committee lay in earlier calls for a review of local authority responsibilities for the personal social services and of the nature of the services provided, particularly in the child care field in the report of the Ingleby Committee (Ingleby, 1960) and the White Paper, *The Child the Family and the Young Offender* (Home Office, 1965). The Seebohm Committee was appointed on 20th December 1965 to 'review the organisation and responsibilities of the local authority personal social services in England and Wales and to consider what changes are desirable to secure an effective family service' (Seebohm, 1968, Para. 1).

The members of the Committee were represented as a group of disinterested experts. As one Director of Social services put it in an interview, they were 'of intellectual stature and sufficiently unprejudiced to be able to examine afresh new approaches to old welfare problems' (Philpot, 1985, p. 17). The alternative view is that the experts were far from disinterested and that social work interests captured the Seebohm Committee and determined the overall thrust of its report, subsequently mounting a successful campaign for implementation (Thomas, 1973: Cooper, 1983). Corrigan and Leonard regard this valuing of the role of supposedly disinterested expertise as characteristic of how change was effected within the social democratic welfare state. The ends of the welfare state were already agreed, only the means were in question. The state was posed against the market as a strong institution within which welfare needs could be met. Welfare reforms were formulated within state institutions with a heavy input from professional and political elites (Corrigan and Leonard, 1978, p. 143). The Seebohm Committee was thus part of a social democratic tradition of bringing in experts to formulate proposals for structural reorganisation.

The Committee's Report was published in July 1968. Its detailed implications for the promotion of the bureau-professional form of the social work labour process are considered in the next section. Here its social democratic commitment to citizenship rights, enshrined in universal services, is explored. The Committee regarded universalism as the antidote to the stigma and paternalism of administrative functions and categories of need, stemming back to the Poor Law, but which the Committee thought were still associated with existing forms of local authority social work. In overturning the Poor Law legacy, the Committee sought to transform the personal social services into a 'commonweal' organisation (Blau and Scott, 1963, p. 43), with the general public as beneficiary

> We recommend a new local authority department, providing a community-based and family-oriented service, which will be available to all. This new department will, we believe, reach far beyond the discovery and rescue of social casualties; it will enable the greatest possible number of individuals to act reciprocally, giving and receiving service for the well-being of the community (Seebohm, 1968, Para. 2).

The universalist tone of the report was nowhere more apparent than in the deliberations of the Committee on the question of what is a family?: 'We decided very early in our discussions that it would be impossible to restrict our work solely to the needs of two or even three generation families. We could only make sense of our task by considering also childless couples and individuals without any close relatives: in other words, everybody' (Seebohm, 1968, Para. 32). The universalist tone of the Report was complemented by a stress on comprehensiveness. Provision of community services was to be comprehensive in scope (Webb and Wistow, 1987, p. 64). Prior to Seebohm the state had accumulated incrementally responsibilities for specific problems. Seebohm envisaged a full-blooded, generalised social democratic responsibility for the social problems of the citizenry (Joyce et al., 1988, p. 48): 'One single department concerned with most aspects of 'welfare' as the public generally understands the term is an essential first step in making services more easily accessible. They must not be camouflaged by administrative complexity, or their precise responsibilities closely defined on the basis of twenty year old statutes' (Seebohm, 1968, Para. 146). Universalism and comprehensiveness were to be pursued proactively through the Social Services Departments' involvement in social planning and social change. Services were to be extended through the planned matching of resources to local needs sought out through research, with the community having a key role in defining needs and shaping services (Webb and Wistow, 1987, p. 217).

Following the Report's publication, social work activists worked as a coherent political force through the Seebohm Implementation Action Group to promote their professional agenda and interests in a campaign for the adoption of the Seebohm proposals (Hall, 1976, p. 108). A Bill was introduced into Parliament in February 1970, without having been preceded by a White Paper or Green Paper. With all party support, the Local Authority Social Services Act was placed unamended on the statute book on 29th May 1970, the last day in office of the

Labour Government, and implemented by the Heath Government which came to power three weeks later. The Act to be implemented was a 'slim dry technical document' (Hallett, 1982, p. 22). The Act was technical in the sense that it was only concerned with the changes in local government which were necessary in order to accommodate the establishment of Social Services Departments, (the appointment of Chief Officers and the setting up of Social Services Committees), and with itemising the legislative responsibilities the new Departments would inherit from their predecessor departments. It provided a loose overall framework, but no philosophy or purposes, within which to build a uniform and unified organisational structure from previously dispersed services (Webb and Wistow, 1987. p. 57; Cooper, 1991). Local authorities were to appoint Directors of Social Services by January 1971 and to complete implementation of the new structure by April 1971. No stipulations were made about internal departmental structures. Organisational structures were to be the product of local decisions. Following implementation, the D.H.S.S.'s 1972 Ten Year Plan assumed growth in real terms of 10% p.a. (D.H.S.S., 1971). In fact the growth peaked in 1973/4 at 20% (D.H.S.S., 1976).

 The developments set out above represent the consolidation of social work's position as part of the post-war social democratic welfare state. They have been described as the 'high tide of social work', coming at the tail-end of the commitment of 1960s social democracy to tackling the problems of society through expertise located in the state and promoting citizenship through solidarity (Langan, 1993, p. 48). The next section considers the manifestation of social work in this social democratic context in the form of a bureau-professional organisational structure.

The bureau-professional organisational structure of the social work labour process

Clarke and Newman stress the significance of internal regimes of bureau-professionalism within the welfare state (Clarke and Newman, 1993, p. 49). Such regimes combine two key aspects of the organisation of state welfare; the rational administration of bureaucratic systems and professional expertise in control over the content of services (Clarke and Langan, 1993b, p. 67). Bureau-professionalism is a specific configuration of structures, cultures, relationships and processes of organisational co-ordination which nevertheless is shaped by location in specific contexts, for example social work's base in local government (Newman and Clarke, 1994, pp. 22-23). Parry and Parry emphasise the extent to which, in the implementation of the Seebohm Report, reorganisation of the personal social services and professional unification came together in an affirmation of both managerial structures and claims for professionalism:

In 1970 the new Social Services Departments came into being; they represented the culmination of post-war developments in social work involving, as they did, a blending of elements of professionalism and bureaucratic organisation. Neither autonomous professionalism nor purely bureaucratic hierarchies emerged from the reorganisation. Instead the new departments were a conflation of both elements, manifesting something of the strains and complexities which such a mixture involves. This mode of organisation...is a hybrid, which we shall refer to as bureau-professionalism...It involved a negotiated partnership between social work, attempting to organise as a profession on the one hand, and the managerial and organisational approach of the state and local authorities on the other (Parry and Parry, 1979, pp. 42-43).

The implementation of the Seebohm Report required, therefore, the creation of a labour process which was neither built on the work of autonomous professionals (Glastonbury et al., 1982) nor constructed as a bureaucracy with functionaries but premised on the merging of social work's professional identity with the personal social services' organisational structure. As a consequence, social work established a structurally independent position from other occupations (Hugman, 1991, p. 7): 'The formation of Social Services Departments ...was widely acknowledged as marking a new dawn for social work. Freed from its previous subordination to the medical profession and with official sanction for its individualised treatment philosophy, it seemed as though the long struggle to gain recognition and a slice of the welfare state of its own had been successful' (Jones, 1983, p. 3). The Seebohm Report regarded social work as central to the new Social Services Departments (Satyamurti, 1981, p. 15) and whilst the departments were not synonymous with social work, and social workers were a minority of the total numbers of staff, the new departments were immediately and fully absorbed in social work's preoccupations (Webb and Wistow, 1987, p. 59; Cooper, 1991). Social work was to exist not as simply another branch of local authority administration but in its own right as the professional/managerial negotiated order represented by bureau-professionalism. A common professional identity was forged through the bringing together of social work's previous sub-groupings and a common training in the skills needed for the newly fashionable generic practice (Webb and Wistow, 1987, pp. 46-52).

The Seebohm Committee's Report contained two distinct elements on which to build the bureau-prcfessional structure of the social work labour process: centralisation and decentralisation. The second element was developed much further in the Report than the first. Decentralisation was seen as necessary and desirable, whereas centralisation rested on the residual need for a framework of centrally determined priorities within which decentralised services would be located, with decentralised management (Challis, 1990, p. 86). Hence the Seebohm Report recommended '...the backing of these community based area units by strong comprehensive resources provided by strong local authorities' (Seebohm,

1968, Para. 605). The Seebohm Committee's case for a strong central presence rested on the power the new departments would be able to wield in local authorities: 'Within local councils a committee responsible for the whole range of the personal social services would rank as a major committee' (Seebohm, 1968, Para 150). But throughout the Report the key to successful reorganisation of the personal social services was seen to lie in decentralisation. The Report gave strong support to the case for decentralised offices staffed by professional social workers: 'We attach great importance to the comprehensive area team approach in the search for an effective family social service and, as a concomitant, the delegation of the maximum authority for decisions to the area office' (Seebohm, 1968, Para 392). Geographical decentralisation, and the accompanying delegation of functions and power from the centre to the periphery, was presented as the first and foremost element in attaining service user-oriented objectives: 'All the personal social services should be located under one roof wherever possible and they should be decentralised to bring them nearer to the public and make them more accessible' (Seebohm, 1968, Para. 108) ... 'with the maximum amount of responsibility delegated to them from the headquarters of the social service department' (Seebohm, 1968, Para. 19).

The discussion of decentralisation in the Report remained at a general level of enthusiasm, with no specific models being advocated: 'There can be no standard pattern for these area offices' (Seebohm, 1968, Para. 588); 'There will have to be considerable flexibility in the kind of organisation adopted, the size of the area and the population served, and the size and composition of the area team to take account of the differing patterns of need in different areas' (Seebohm, 1968, Para. 591). As we saw in the previous section the Local Authority Social Services Act (1970) left local authorities to decide on organisational structures. The Committee contented itself with portraying a general picture of an Area Team led by a senior professional responsible for a specific population in a defined geographical area. Such teams were a key and distinctive feature of the social work labour process.

Conclusion: the social work labour process reconsidered

Having considered the social democratic context and content of the Seebohm Report, made manifest in the advocacy of a bureau-professional organisational structure, the overall configuration of the social work labour process can now be reconsidered. In Derber's terms, the developments on the one hand extended the technical autonomy of social workers. On the other hand the settlement in state/professional work relations, represented by the institutional arrangements of bureau-professionalism, was accompanied by the continued ideological subordination of social workers. This was achieved through social work's location in the legislative, fiscal and organisational base of the welfare state as the political framework within which the social work labour process was structured.

In contrast, the review of the radical social work literature in Chapter Three showed that the radical critique of the Seebohm reorganisation was concentrated on the technical subordination of social workers through the bureaucratic managerial facet of the bureau-professional labour process within which social work was located. The assumption in the radical social work literature was that the bureaucratic managerial facet represented a threat to social work through its propensity to exert (technical) control: 'In this changed and changing context, local authorities do not welcome social workers who believe themselves to be virtuoso professionals, who feel that they should have the right exclusively to control their work. On many issues a powerful professional social work culture rests uneasily with local government bureaucracies' (Jones, 1983, p. 132); 'The reorganisation of social services into large departments within the structure of local authorities continually threatens to bureaucratise and depersonalise a personal service' (Bailey and Brake, 1980, p. 11).

Webb and Wistow question these assumptions. They accept that, after a short-lived debate about the appropriateness of a bureaucratic hierarchy in a community-oriented professionally-staffed service, the implementation of the Seebohm Report led to the establishment of hierarchies in the new Departments. However, they stress that such an organisational arrangement is a system of accountability upwards and delegation downwards which does not automatically nor necessarily mean that workers are closely or authoritarianally controlled with very little discretion. They argue the converse: a bureaucratic hierarchy of accountability is compatible with considerable discretion and that with such discretion hierarchy need not be synonymous with rigidity (Webb and Wistow, 1987, pp. 107-108). For example, they point to the survival of the casework tradition in Social Services Departments, despite the questioning and debate which surrounded it in the post-Seebohm period (Webb and Wistow, 1987, p. 60). In similar vein, Hugman identifies the possibility that bureaucracy might allow the scope of professional work to develop. The implementation of the Seebohm Report, for example, delivered resources which consolidated social work's control over its area of work (Hugman, 1991, p. 78), as we have seen. Accordingly, bureaucratic hierarchies can be as much a basis for the power exercised by professionals as the basis for the exercise of power over professionals (Hugman, 1991, p. 62). What all this suggests, is that it is hazardous to read off a presumed labour process, along the lines of the orthodox Bravermanian industrial model, from the existence of a hierarchical structure in the way the radical social work writers appeared to have done. The precise structuring of the social work labour process needs to be identified along with the processes taking place within it: 'In practice,...less is formalised, prescribed and regulated within Social Services Departments than might be imagined from an uncritical response to and antagonism against "the bureaucracy" ' (Hallet, 1982, p. 49).

In the light of the foregoing discussion of the Seebohm Report's implementation in the political context of the social democratic welfare state, it is difficult to establish the direct link between social work and industrial capitalist labour processes, alluded to by radical social writers. As we have seen the attempt to establish citizenship rights within the personal social services predominated over the desire to set up 'Seebohm factories'. The radical social work writers were attempting to break the hold of social democratic ideology by revealing it as a smoke-screen obscuring the capture of Social Services Departments by capitalist rationality (Bolger et al., 1981, pp. 45-47). On the contrary, with social democracy as the political context and bureau-professionalism as the organisational structure no great imperative existed to extend, in Derber's terms, ideological subordination into technical subordination. This becomes clear in the account of the levels in social work's bureau-professional state labour process, presented in the next chapter.

5 Levels in the social work labour process

Introduction

Having stressed the importance of locating the social work labour process within the state and explored the distinctiveness of state-mediated professional work, Chapter Four gave an account of the consolidation of the bureau-professional structure of the social work labour process in the social democratic welfare state.

Later chapters draw on a case study of 'Welfareville' Social Services Department and focus particularly on the front-line manager's position in the labour process. Before moving in that specific direction, in this chapter a more rounded account of the social work labour process is provided. Brown suggests that such accounts have been absent from the labour process perspective because of its narrow preoccupation with the 'frontier of control' (Brown, 1992, p.222). Notwithstanding, therefore, the importance of the pivotal position of the front-line manager in the social work labour process, in the interests of giving a rounded account of the social work labour process it is now suggested that the social work labour process of the late 1970s/early 1980s was stratified on a number of levels:

- Central government,
- Local government,
- Middle management,
- Front-line management,
- Social worker/service user contact.

Each of these levels is considered in turn.

Central government

The representation of the social work labour process which follows depicts it as stratified on a number of different levels, each of which is relatively autonomous. At one extremity of these levels is central government, producing the personal social services' legislative mandate. Legislation in the form of the Local Authority Social Services Act (1970) both established Social Services Departments and, reinforced by other pieces of legislation, imposed statutory duties upon them. The social work labour process is initiated by central government legislation. Central government-derived statutory duties are the framework within which social work is practised. Legislation embodies particular perspectives on the way people with 'problems' and 'needs' are defined and, in general terms, outlines the ways in which Social Services Departments can respond to them, including the amount of power and control Social Services Departments can exercise over service users. Social Services Departments are the sites through which central government legislation is filtered and turned into concrete policies and practices.

Discussing the central government level of the social work labour process in these terms runs the risk of setting up a 'line of command' model in which central government simply gives instructions to local authority Social Services Departments through legislation. However, it is clear that there was not a single coherent set of policies for the personal social services in the late 1970s/early 1980s, but rather streams of policy interacting, sometimes in contradictory ways (Webb and Wistow, 1987, p. 130). These policy streams were promulgated through a variety of channels and arenas: the legislation itself, White Papers, policy documents, Ministers' remarks and guidelines, resource planning processes. In this fluid set of relationships the Seebohm Report argued successfully for the clarification of the main channel from central government to the personal social services: 'There must be one central government department responsible for the relationship between central government and the social service departments ...to provide the overall national planning of social services, social intelligence and social research' (Seebohm, 1968, Para. 637). That central government department was the Department of Health and Social Security, created in 1968. However, whilst the other services falling within the D.H.S.S., the National Health Service and Social Security, were directly accountable to the Secretary of State, local authorities were not directly managerially accountable to central government for the personal social services. As a consequence the National Health Service and Social Security had uniform structures and a set of national policies, but the personal social services did not; local government led to local variation (Webb and Wistow, 1987, p. 3). The systems of accountability for the services falling within the D.H.S.S.'s remit varied. Social Security was run by civil servants responsible to the Secretary of State. In the case of the N.H.S., Regional Health Authorities were agents of the Secretary of State but with the Secretary of State still accountable for the running of the National Health Service. The Secretary of State had much less direct responsibility for the personal social services. Under Section 7 of the Local Authority Social Services Act 1970, local authorities were to 'act under the general guidance of the Secretary of State'.

The Secretary of State articulated this guidance through general policy frameworks, with advice to and monitoring of Social Services Departments through the D.H.S.S.'s Social Work Advisory Service. The Social Work Advisory Service's work had a lightness of touch in this era, compared to its approach in its new identity as the Social Services Inspectorate from 1986 onwards. The Social Work Advisory Service's low-key approach was consistent with the recommendations of the Seebohm Committee: 'We see the role of the Inspectorate as not so much regulatory as promotional, educational and consultative'. According to the Committee, what was needed was a 'strong, accessible and well-respected Inspectorate to advise local authorities, to promote the achievement of aims and the maintenance of standards, and to act as two-way channels for information and consultation between central and local government' (Seebohm, 1968, Para. 647). A form of peer review was envisaged with 'free movement between the central government Inspectorate and local authority services encouraged' (Seebohm, 1968, Para. 649). When the Social Work Advisory Service was established in 1971, the circular announcing its arrival retained faithfully the Seebohm Report's emphasis on advice and consultation. The Social Work Advisory Service was 'to advise local authorities, to promote the achievement of aims and the maintenance of standards and to act as two-way channels for information and consultation between central and local government' (Hallett, 1982, p. 88).

In the late 1970s/early 1980s, there was then no direct line of command from central government dictating either the organisational structure of the social work labour process at the local authority level or the detailed policies implemented within and through that structure. There was a relationship between two relatively autonomous levels in the labour process. Within, by later standards, loose overall financial controls, there was room for local authority Social Services Departments to shape structures and policies within central government's general policy guidance.

Local government

Corporate management

The establishment of Social Services Departments in 1971 occurred in the wider context of the adoption of 'corporate management' in local government and the organisational structures erected for the implementation of the Seebohm Report were caught up in the discourse of corporatism. As corporatism took hold of debates about local authority structures, Benington (1976) and Cockburn (1977) argue that corporate management was introduced into local political structures as a management system from private capital in order to achieve centralised control. Both writers argue that the introduction of corporate management in local government was used to achieve detailed control over all aspects of corporate functioning, and thence outwards to control the communities being served. Bolger et al draw on Benington and Cockburn to represent the shift to corporate management as the impetus behind the trend towards an industrial model of management in social work: 'This form of control, taken from capital itself, was adopted by various committees appointed to examine all aspects of public accountability and government. The overall tendency throughout was to adopt centralised and hierarchical modes of management found in capitalist enterprises' (Bolger et al, 1981, p. 57). Corporate management is thus regarded as the structure which facilitated the introduction of private sector management techniques. These techniques are seen as further strengthening 'the centralised mode of control':

> The total effect of these changes in the structure of the local state was to centralise control and policy formulation...the centralised control of management...has directly reduced [local authority workers'] autonomy...The feelings of increased powerlessness experienced daily within Social Services Departments are based upon a real structural centralisation which has shifted power not only away from the base within the Department, but from the Department to the Policy Advisory Committee (Bolger et al, 1981, pp. 58-59).

Whilst it is undoubtedly the case that up until the early 1980s structural issues dominated debates about management in local government and organisational principles from the private sector were used to restructure local government (Smith et al, 1991, p. 2), it is nevertheless important to introduce the note of caution sounded by Smith et al about the degree of fit that was achieved between private industry and local government:

> Because of the non-capitalist nature of some public sector organisations, capitalist solutions must always be a half measure, an approximate fit, contested and competing with a service ideology and wider political practices that go beyond the criteria of profitability...When examining work within the public sector it is important to incorporate an awareness of its distinctive characteristics (Smith et al, 1991, p. 3).

This can be illustrated through a consideration of the circumstances in which corporate management was introduced, the extent to which corporate management was achieved and corporate management's attendant contradictions.

From the 1960s onwards the need to reorganise the organisational structures of local government was the source of considerable debate. Existing local authority Departments were depicted as insular, jealously guarding their specialist responsibilities through senior professionals linked into national policy networks. The management of departments by professional experts and administrators was the antithesis of the council-wide approach to management sought for by the corporate reformers (Cochrane, 1994, p. 144). The managerial reforms were 'aimed at creating administrative and management systems in place of what were identified as archaic and ramshackle systems which had developed over the previous 150 years and whose lack of integration presented a major stumbling block to the efficient co-ordination and management of public services' (Clarke and Langan, 1993a, p. 41). Although attempts at reform had gathered pace from the 1960s onwards (Leach et al, 1994, pp. 26-29), it was the reorganisation of local government in 1974, with the setting up of new local authorities, which provided the opportunity of tackling what was regarded as petty departmentalism (Cochrane, 1994, p. 145). It was believed that larger authorities responsible for the bulk of service provision would result in more effective management through the public sector adaptation of private business wisdom.   Large private sector corporations with corporate management systems were regarded as the best integrated and most cost-effective organisational form. Such corporations provided the model for developing local government approaches to long-term planning and the efficient allocation of resources (Clarke and Langan, 1993, pp. 43-44; Cochrane, 1994, p. 145).

The Bains Report (1972) provided the basis for the management structure and processes to be adopted following the 1974 local government reorganisation. In implementing that reorganisation three common elements appeared in local government: A Policy and Resources Committee with responsibility for authority-wide policies and bargaining about resource allocation; a reduced number of service committees and departments with wider remits, compared with the 1950s and 1960s, a trend which began with the creation of Social Services Departments; a chief executive convening a management team of chief officers to discuss authority-wide or cross-departmental issues and to advise the Policy and Resources Committee. These elements were seized upon by Benington (1976) (and by Bolger et al, 1981, see above), as evidence of dramatic changes in the management of local government.

Although these three common elements of a corporate management approach were put in place, local structures and practices varied considerably within the framework provided by them (Elcock, 1993, p. 153). Several writers argue that it is all too easy to exaggerate the significance of corporate management as a sharp break with the past. Surviving within the facade of corporate management was the bureaucratic paternalism characteristic of the post-war social democratic consensus (Crewe, 1982; Hoggett and Hambleton, 1987), with corporate management as an outward semblance of co-ordination in the formulation of long-term strategy (Webb and Wistow, 1987, p. 219). By the late 1970s, the original structures erected to pursue corporate management were regarded as too cumbersome and were in decline (Greenwood et al, 1980).   Attempts at full-blooded, private sector corporation-style management were short-lived (in the sense of on-going management of the full range of activities across the local authority), as the power of individual departments, and their links into national policy networks, was reasserted. What remained was a corporate planning cycle for setting general objectives and reviewing progress towards them, which did not challenge existing local authority assumptions (Leach et al., 1994, p. 33). Leach et al. conclude that the corporate management approach in local government was solely concerned with the extent to which the 'building blocks were moved about', leaving local authority strategies and cultures untouched (Leach et al., 1994, pp. 70-72): 'The degree of real change was limited, reflecting the difference between the relative ease of changing the structure of the organisation and the much greater difficulty of changing the culture. The new positions and approaches were added to the traditional system rather than the system being transformed' (Leach et al., 1994, p. 109). In this context, the corporate planning cycle provided a site for negotiations between chief officers over resource allocation, through the traditional incremental budgetary process. On that site, the contest waged was over the allocation of growth to departments, not corporate direction (Cochrane, 1994, pp. 146-148): 'Although the language of general local government acts and constitutional discussion tended to define local authorities as unitary multi-functional agencies, the closer one moved to the practice of individual departments the less appropriate such a construction appeared' (Cochrane, 1994, p. 151). This was particularly the case for Social Services Departments which were engaged in marking out their distinctiveness in local government.

The preceding discussion suggests the need for caution in any assessment of the precise impact of corporate management on the local government level of the social work labour process. But we can go further. A contradiction bound up with corporate management's transference from the private sector into the public sector concerns its potential to further politicise local government, a contradiction unexplored in the view of local government having become 'big business' (Benington, 1976). The tendency towards greater politicisation stemmed from the attempt at greater co-ordination and integration within corporate management. Departmental fragmentation, poor co-ordination of policies and service provision and the inefficient use of resources were issues which needed to be addressed in local government in this era (Greenwood and Stewart, 1974; Joyce et al., 1988, p. 62), if differentiation and departmentalism 'were to be matched by mechanisms capable of integrating the work of the authority' (Greenwood, 1983, p. 167; and see Elcock, 1993). As a consequence of the attempt at greater integration, there were pressures for increased acceptance of a *governmental* role by local authorities (Greenwood and Stewart, 1974). A subsequently neglected emphasis in the Bains Report is that given to the need to shift from local administration to local government:

Local government is not, in our view limited to the narrow provision of a series of services to the local community, though we do not intend in any to suggest that these services are not important. It has within its purview the overall economic, cultural and physical well-being of that community and for this reason its decisions impinge with increasing frequency upon the individual life of its citizens (Bains Report, 1972, p. 6).

In similar vein, the Maud Report had earlier called for the relaxation of specific statutory duties on local authorities in favour of granting general competence to them to undertake what in their opinion was in the interests of their areas and their inhabitants (Maud Report, 1967, Paras. 200, 607-608). Rather than obscuring politics in business management approaches (Benington, 1976), it can be argued that through these injunctions to local authorities to reject seeing themselves as simply carrying out the functions allotted to them by central government and to accept the need for local government to have a wider responsibility for the communities they served,   corporate management had a contradictory tendency to prompt greater politicisation at the local level.

The 1970s appeared to be a time of major change in the local government level of the social work labour process. In retrospect, the amount of change which took place in the operating environment for social work was small. With the benefit of hindsight, the significance of corporate management was overrated and its implementation overstated.

Social work in local government

In the 1970s and early 1980s, local authorities interpreted central government legislation, mediating between it and service users (Cooper, 1991). Social work was not only a state labour process it was also a labour process constructed in a local political context. The Seebohm Committee envisaged '... the organisational structure of a social service department within a dynamic democratic local government system' (Seebohm, 1968, Para. 581). Locating the reconstructed personal social services firmly within local government was at the heart of the Committee's view of their potential effectiveness through local accountability: '"Effectiveness" in terms of a democratically controlled local government service implies a service with assured communication between the "consumer" of the service and those responsible for policy and the provision of the necessary resources' (Seebohm, 1968, Para. 582). Local government provided not just a system of accountability for the personal social services, it also provided the potential for local choice (Stewart, 1983). Local authorities were providers of services, under statute, but they were also political institutions which had the capacity to vary their structures, procedures and the form and level of the services they provided (Stewart, 1983, p. vi). The internal management of departments was officer- dominated, with professional cultures of technical expertise (Stewart,

1983, p. 18; Stewart, 1989, p. 174; Challis, 1990, p. 6; Laffin and Young, 1990, p. 24). Webb and Wistow suggest that within Social Services Departments, as local authority policy sub-systems (Webb and Wistow, 1987, p. 63), the complexity of the issues and professional autonomy further increased the power of senior officers (Webb and Wistow, 1987, p. 64).

Thus, the nature of the social work labour process at the local government level was not specified in detail by central government. Central government was dependent on local government to interpret and implement legislation, with senior managers advising councillors on policies, procedures and resources required to implement legislation in the political context of local conditions. Within the political process of local government councillors and senior managers elaborated policies, allocated resources and instituted procedures to comply with statutory duties: 'The autonomy of the [local authority] employing body derives from the freedom with which they can organise their own social services' (Howe, 1986a, p. 161). For example, when local authorities implemented the Seebohm Report, they were not required to straightforwardly apply one detailed model of the structure of the social work labour process. Choices had to be made about the detailed structuring of the labour process at the local level (Challis, 1990). Further, as we saw in the previous section, in this period central government policy guidance on the implementation of specific legislation through the social work labour process was couched in general terms.

For the Seebohm Committee, constructing the social work labour process through local government placed a dual responsibility on social workers to service users and management (Webb and Wistow, 1987, p. 99). As an alternative approach, Webb and Wistow identify three facets of Social Services' Departments multiple accountability:

    i.   to individual service users;
    ii.   to the whole population of actual and potential service users;
    iii.   to the public purse for cost-effectiveness (Webb and Wistow, 1987, p. 104).

They suggest that this multiple accountability of Departments can be tackled through two different approaches:

    a)   Social workers wholly accountable to individual service users [i] and the Department as a whole bearing responsibility for the whole population of actual and potential service users [ii] and to the public purse for cost- effectiveness [iii]. In order to achieve [ii] and [iii] social workers' discretion in their work with individual service users [i] must be constrained by rules or procedures to safeguard use of resources and to attempt fair distribution of them between all service users and potential service users.

b)   Social workers responsible for all three facets [i, ii and iii] of accountability and for keeping their responsibilities for all three facets in balance (Webb and Wistow, 1987, p. 105).

Within a social democratic political framework the bureau-professional organisational form of the social work labour process is a way of trying to square this three-fold accountability in line with approach a). There is considerable professional discretion at the level of social worker/service user contact [i] (this level is dealt with later in the chapter) and bureaucratic accountability to local politicians, through managers who were previously social workers, for [ii] and [iii]. (In contrast, radical social work writers stress the overriding duty of social workers to be solely responsible to service users' interests [i] as presented to them, setting aside [ii] and [iii]). The lament not just from radical social work writers but from a range of opinion for unfettered professional freedom of action for social workers thus misses the point about multiple accountability in a local political system: 'If social workers wish to argue for complete professional independence the logical step must be to provide such a service without public money and without public control' (Webb and Wistow, 1987, p. 113).

Within local political systems, Stewart concludes that relationships at the councillor-senior manager level in this period were both deeply political and deeply professional. Within legislative constraints local authorities could make policy choices about the activities undertaken (and the extent and form of them) and organisational choices (on structures, practices and procedures). Within the councillor-senior officer modus vivendi such choices might be influenced by the political complexion of the local authority (for example, the choices made by a Labour local authority in a northern mining town, and those made by a Conservative London borough), or the professional complexion of chief officers (for example, an innovator as opposed to a bureaucrat) (Stewart, 1983, p. 18).

Middle management

In the previous section, the concentration was on politicians and senior managers at the level of the labour process designated for the purpose of this discussion as 'local government', the level of those engaged in longer-term policy and planning within political and financial constraints. The next section considers the front-line management level of the labour process, which is the particular focus of the case study of 'Welfareville' Social Services Department in later chapters. Between the front-line management level in the labour process and the local government level was a middle stratum of management concerned with the interaction between the local government level of policy and planning and management decisions taken at the front-line level. At this intermediate level, middle managers with geographically-based and/or specialism-based responsibilities co-ordinated the implementation of policy and allocated resources in accordance with senior managers' interpretation of the Department's legislative responsibilities and councillors' political priorities.

Front-line management

The Seebohm Committee placed the front-line unit it proposed, the Area Team, at the centre of its plans for the restructuring of the personal social services. It envisaged considerable autonomy for this level in the labour process, rather than the direction of the work of Area Teams by senior, centrally-based management or by middle managers: 'The important points are that the social service department can only work effectively through area teams, drawing support from the communities they serve, with a *substantial measure of delegated authority to take decisions*, and able to call on the more specialised resources, advice and support of the departmental headquarters when the need arises' (Seebohm, 1968, Para. 594). The Committee emphasised the functional autonomy it regarded as essential to the new departments in its proposal for the management of the Area Teams:

> We attach great importance to the comprehensive area team approach in the search for an effective family social service and, as a concomitant, *the delegation of the maximum authority for decisions to the area offices...* We suggest that ideally each area office should be controlled by a senior professionally trained social worker with a grasp of administrative issues and wide powers of decision (Seebohm, 1968, para. 592).

Seebohm himself chose to push home the point at the press conference which launched the Committee's report: 'We attach great importance to this decentralisation, which is not just physically moving them [social workers] out from the centre and putting them into area units, but also involves a great deal of delegation of decision-making. I think this is the only way to make an effective service on the ground' (From press conference transcript, 1968, reprinted in Seebohm, 1989, pp. 2-3).

There is a literature on 'task discontinuous organisations' (Clegg and Dunkerley, 1980, pp. 474-476, Howe, 1986, pp. 110-113) and 'front-line organisations' (Hallett, 1982, p. 51) which argues for the distinctiveness of the type of organisation proposed by the Seebohm Committee. In a front-line organisation 'organisational initiative is located in the front-line unit; each unit performs independently of others with obstacles to the direct supervision of units' work' (Smith in Hallett, 1982, p. 51). Payne identifies three factors which have a bearing on how powerful a front-line unit is likely to be in relation to senior management:

geographical distance from headquarters; population size; and number of staff (Payne, 1979, pp. 98-100).

The available evidence suggests that front-line managers were able to exploit the autonomy proposed for area teams by the Seebohm Committee. Satyamurti found in her study of a London borough's Social Services Department that front-line managers did not view the wider department as an object to which they owed loyalty or with which they identified. There was little scrutiny of their work and they could disregard specific departmental rules without negative consequences. She found that there was considerable latitude in how they made up their role, for example, the extent to which they were involved in practice (Satyamurti, 1981, p. 35).

Parsloe, drawing on the findings of research into the practice of 33 area teams, concludes:

> Sometimes we felt that a kind of Berlin wall existed between each team and every other part of the department within which it was situated. It was particularly high and well-guarded between teams and what members always called "the hierarchy", which meant everyone above team leaders...It was apparent that, in general, management had laid down few policy guidelines for the way teams undertook their work. Decisions about the way duty, intake and allocation were managed seemed to be made by the teams themselves... Teams often appeared to make decisions in a vacuum which was seldom filled by guidance from headquarters (Parsloe, 1981, pp. 92-93).

Parsloe also identifies the permissive culture which existed behind the 'Berlin Wall', in particular the absence of detailed forms or guidelines to make assessments; no shared criteria for deciding who in the team should do what work; no shared ideas about the kind or amount of work members should undertake: 'In other words, they [teams] lacked common instruments for assessment, work planning, work allocation and case and workload management...Team leaders sometimes had a list of their workers' cases' (Parsloe, 1981, p. 60). Parsloe notes that as far as the front-line manager's role was concerned, goals were stated in global terms and seldom made explicit; that only one team of the 33 studied worked within an explicit framework of agency priorities; that seldom were methods of work laid down by senior management and that teams had considerable scope for changing the ways in which they worked (Parsloe, 1981, p. 129).

Pithouse's study of the operation of one area office demonstrates the scope for front-line managers to manage in such a way as to prevent close scrutiny by more senior managers. Local managers controlled the exchange of information between themselves and the rest of the Department. Pithouse stresses the negotiable working arrangements which emerged in the area office from the initiative of participants, rather than through formal rules or objectives. Social workers and front-line managers saw themselves as definers of good practice as a result of the insulation of the area office from the rest of the department (Pithouse, 1987, pp. 47-49).   Pithouse comments that in this insulated context 'good' front-line managers 'demonstrate to their teams their independence from higher management, and their disinclination to intrude overly in social workers' day to day practices' (Pithouse, 1987, p. 64).

The combined weight of these research findings contrasts sharply with the assertions in the radical social work literature (see Chapter Three) that powerful new managerial controls had been introduced in field social work teams.

Social worker/service user contact

In the labour process levels considered thus far, central government has been identified as the originator of legislation and general policy developments; local government has been seen as the political and managerial context in which those general policies are fleshed out and implemented; and the characteristics of the middle and front-line levels of management have been explored. It is at the final level of the social work labour process that social workers are expected to identify individuals' problems and needs and work with them within the statutory framework of the social work labour process.

Challis argues that at the social worker/service user level Social Services Departments' implementation of central government legislation requires professional expertise. Social workers, she stresses, have to have a degree of discretion and autonomy if they are to deal with the idiosyncrasies of people's lives and therefore their dealings are regulated not by bureaucratic procedures but views of what constitutes professional practice (Challis, 1990, p. 6). This is an apt starting point for consideration of this final level of the labour process. The central point to be made is that the nature of social work in the late 1970s/early 1980s did not render it as susceptible to managerial control - in Derber's sense of technical subordination (see Chapter Four) - as the radical social work literature suggested (see Chapter Three). In the radical social work literature the failure to distinguish first, between different levels in the labour process and second, between ideological and technical subordination resulted in the assumption that increased control of social worker/service user contact had subordinated the social worker to managerial control. However, within the social work labour process the potential for technical subordination by managers was limited because of the unpredictable nature of the work and because the basis of social work is in face-to-face contact with service users beyond management scrutiny. Social workers, as we will see in Chapter Eight, were supervised by front-line managers who had to rely on indirect access to social workers' practice through social workers' own accounts of their work. Thus, social workers maintained immediate control over this level of the labour process (vis-à-vis managers). Direct monitoring by managers was rarely feasible. Social workers had command over their time and at the point of contact with service users decided how much time to give and how it was used, the frequency with which they would meet service users, the strategy to be adopted with people with whom they were working and even, in some cases, whether they would provide a service at all. Social workers had the freedom not only to interpret rules, for example whether a service user fitted a particular category, but also to define problems and the priority to be allocated to them.

Examples of such elements of wide-ranging discretion in social work can be drawn from a number of sources, for example Pearson's notions of social workers as 'professional saboteurs' and 'bandits' (Pearson, 1973; 1975) and Lipsky's consideration of the work of 'street level bureaucrats', those people working in a bureaucracy who have the front-line responsibility to work with the public and carry out the policies of the organisation. According to Lipsky, street level bureaucrats develop a style of work which makes their own practice manageable and they choose which aspects of policies to emphasise: ....'the decisions of street level bureaucrats...effectively become the public policies they carry out...Street level bureaucrats have discretion because the nature of service provision calls for human judgement...' (Lipsky, 1980, p. 104). Satyamurti makes a similar point from her study of a Social Services Department: 'For social workers... statutory duties were the framework within which their objectives were formulated; to the director they may constitute the objectives themselves' (Satyamurti, 1981, p. 23).

Challis identifies field social workers' roles as gatekeepers to resources as another area of discretion (Challis, 1990, p. 68). She suggests that the criteria for how this function is performed varied from team to team, but the function was constant, giving social workers a great deal of control over the extent to which, and the way in which, services were used. This, she argues, is because social workers have to be able to deal with the non-routine, which requires discretion and autonomy. Social workers may be charged in a general sense with the exercise of statutory duties and powers but they decide how a particular statute is to be interpreted in practice or whether to invoke legislation at all (Challis, 1990, pp. 68-69). Further the decentralised location of social workers creates an environment in which they can extend the bounds of discretion for example by giving priority to particular types of referrals (Challis, 1990, p. 88).

This discretion and autonomy is embodied in casework: '... despite critical assault...the greatest prestige continues to be ascribed to the main form of practice, namely casework...Casework has a long history as the method of practice in which social workers were trained, and this is allied to the individual organisation of practice in personal caseloads' (Hugman, 1991, p. 98). Similarly, Bamford, as a senior social services manager, points out that the bureaucratic and professional facets of the bureau-professional social work labour process co-existed:

The individual social worker retains a degree of personal decision-making responsibilities substantially greater in terms of the consequences for the client affected by his or her decisions than is true of most occupational groups. While changes in organisational structures have been a characteristic managerial response to problems, the responsibility carried by the individual worker has been little affected (Bamford, 1989, p. 155).

As Satyamurti points out social work was individualised and privatised. Social workers had their 'own' cases (Satyamurti, 1981, p. 185). The duties and powers laid on local authorities were couched in broad terms. By the time the social worker was implementing them they might be hedged about by procedures and requirements but often the work content was no more precise (Satyamurti, 1981, p. 36). Satyamurti found that the defining of objectives, ordering of priorities and specification of tasks was minimal so responsibility for sorting out priorities rested with the social workers in her sample. Social workers responded to service users as they saw fit: 'The absence of clearly defined objectives and policies affected the social workers more than other sections of the department. Their job was the most vague, the least well-defined, the lowest in routine task or administrative content' (Satyamurti, 1981, p. 32). It is this feature of the social work labour process which leads Hallet to conclude that Social Services Departments represented a striking departure from the classic model of a bureaucracy because of the absence of:

> ...a detailed system of rules and regulations for dealing with each case. Indeed, much of the activity in relation to particular cases in Social Services Departments is characterised by a high degree of discretion accorded to or assumed by the individual worker...There is the discretion for the basic grade worker to decide upon the method of intervention, the aims of the work, the frequency of client contact and in many instances although not all, the decision to close the case (Hallet, 1982, p. 47).

Pithouse has painted the most detailed picture of the ways in which social workers safeguarded their autonomy as '...self-regulating practitioners who define their own preferred methods of work within a case-based mode of practice' (Pithouse, 1987, p. 49). He argues that any apparent negative orientation to the employing Department uncovered by his research did not stem from strict regulation but rather was a form of praise for local arrangements around autonomy (Pithouse, 1987, p. 51; Pithouse, 1991, p. 45). Pithouse cautions that social work organisations do not always impinge upon workers as much as their complaints would indicate:

> Throughout the research there were no administrative directives or schemes advanced that sought to control closely the daily movements and practices that the workers individually produced...They visit consumers according to priorities they set themselves. They apply their own preferred modes of intervention...They ration their time and pace their energies in the light of their own experiences of case requirements...Work does not occur in some standardised and easily

monitored sequence of time and event...There are no formal attempts to check or scrutinise daily practice apart from supervision meetings with the team leader and these occur fortnightly or monthly...It is this basic element of day to day autonomy that workers take for granted. It is the basis on which the job is routinely done (Pithouse, 1991, pp. 45-46).

Pithouse's commentary on practitioner self-regulation, together with the other evidence which has been reviewed, is at odds with the radical social work literature's account of encroaching managerial control. Smith (1981) argues that even in situations where actions are meant to be guided by specific rules such as guidelines, procedures and legislation the 'meaning of the rule is equally determined by the situated actions which are deemed to constitute that rule' (Smith, 1981, p. 62). In this respect, Smith considers several studies of social work practice which suggest that social workers actively contributed to the interpretation of legislation and procedures: 'The feature of all the studies was the wide-ranging freedom which social workers had to choose the style and content of their direct work with clients' (Smith, 1981, p. 64). (The discretionary nature of social work is evident in a number of other studies [Black et al., 1983; Hallett and Stevenson, 1980; Packman et al., 1986; Stevenson, 1989]).
Smith sums up:

First, professionals in the health, welfare and educational services are clearly in a position to make choices about the quality, if not the quantity, of the help that they provide. Second,...the organisational structures of service agencies permit professional and other workers to at least in part 'create' policy through their attitude, ideology and operational strategies. Third, the importance that has been attached to the training of professionals reflects the concern not only with the acquisition of technical skills but also with the powers of discretionary action exercised by those delivering services (Smith, 1981, p. 267).

Conclusion

This chapter has built in more detail on the previous chapter's consideration of the bureau- professional structure of the social work labour process through an elaboration of the levels in the labour process. In contrast to the radical social work writers, who argued for the existence of an orthodox Bravermanian, industrial model of the social work labour process, the case has been advanced that the social work labour process was not subjected to unequivocal managerial control in the late 1970s/early 1980s. Rather it was a complex of bureau-professional processes. Bamford describes the nature of social work's bureau- professional régime:

The way in which the worker uses his or her distinctive personality is not constrained by the agency, management guidance, or the immediate supervisor. That choice extends to decisions about the nature and focus of social work intervention... but the worker's freedom of choice is not absolute. First, there is an obligation to provide some response to the problem presented. Second, the response is conditioned by the resources at the disposal of the agency... Third, in some areas the employing agency may have developed a policy response which shapes the worker's response...   The choice about whether to adopt a behavioural approach to the problem presented, to use family therapy, to develop group work, or conceptualise the problem in a way justifying collective social action to secure changes in public policy is one for the individual worker. The ethos of supervision in social work agencies remains predominantly one of guidance, support and advice... In addition to personal qualities and choice of method of intervention the worker has discretion in reports to courts and other agencies and as part of the review process within the agency. Again, however, the exercise of a free choice is conditioned by agency and societal expectations... but the views expressed and the way in which they are couched will be determined by the social worker's particular perspective (Bamford, 1989, pp. 139-140).

In later chapters, data from a case study of 'Welfareville' Social Services Department are used to test elements of the bureau-professional model of the social work labour process, developed in this chapter and the previous chapter, against the industrial model developed within the radical social work paradigm. The labour process at the front-line management level is considered through front-line managers' accounts of their experiences and understandings (Chapters Seven and Eight).

But first, Chapter Six introduces the case study and the structure of the social work labour process in 'Welfareville' Social Services Department, following the implementation of the Local Authority Social Services Act (1970).

6 'Welfareville': managing state social work in a local labour process

Introduction

As we saw in Chapter Three, in the radical social work literature 'management' was presented as being engaged in wresting control over the work of field social workers. Following the initial representation of this approach in the radical texts, precisely how this industrial model of gaining managerial control was being achieved remained unresearched. In particular no work was undertaken on the role played by front-line managers in wresting control over the social work labour process, nor on how their own work was faring in the alleged managerial push for greater control.

For these reasons, an empirically grounded approach was considered to be important in expanding the labour process framework. The radical social work paradigm's focus on the restructuring of social work needed to be supplemented by an unveiling of the processes which take place within work structures. Attention had to be paid to both the organisational structure of the labour process, in which front-line managers were located, and to how those managers perceived and negotiated the position they held within it. The limitations of the radical social work literature could begin to be overcome first, by identifying the structure of the social work labour process; secondly, by considering the impact of the structure of the labour process on the work of front-line managers; thirdly, by considering how front-line managers interacted with social workers on a day-to-day basis within the structure; fourthly, by considering how the managers made sense of trade unionism from their position in the labour process. In order to hold on to the importance of both structure and process a case study approach to a Social Services Department was adopted. The considerations which influenced the adoption and implementation of a case study approach are outlined in the next section.

The case study approach

A small-scale exploratory case study was undertaken in one Social Services Department, referred to here as 'Welfareville', as a means of grounding consideration of the social work labour process in front-line managers' experiences and understandings, contextualised in an account of the structure of the social work labour process. The case study approach has a considerable history in the study of work and some of the classic studies of the workplace have involved investigation of one or two organisations (Gouldner, 1954; Roy, 1960; Blau, 1963). The case study experienced a period of decline but Salaman argues there is a need for a renaissance of small case studies of different types of workplaces: 'Analysis of this type, which identifies and seeks to understand and explain patterns of informal structuring of workplace relations, is important as a method of understanding organisational structure, process and dynamics. It is thus an essential element in any form of social enquiry into work organisations' (Salaman, 1986, pp. 112-113). As far as the labour process perspective is concerned, Salaman presses the case for opening up the methods used to study work:

> The currently fashionable form of the sociology of work (the Labour Process) demonstrates an interest in a theoretical focus on the design of work...It is not, therefore, particularly concerned with informal patterns of relationships. Yet it should be. For since the Labour Process is increasingly required to temper the simplicity of Braverman's thesis with the ornamentation of qualification, it finds it necessary to draw upon (or assume) concepts such as strategy, resistance, consciousness, which can only develop within a context of actors' (or agents') conceptions of, feelings about, and objectives of, their work. Once this is granted, the Labour Process...must take seriously and investigate the ways in which employees' worlds of meaning, understanding and evaluation are in fact constructed (Salaman, 1986, p. 113).

Salaman is critical of work within the labour process perspective which represents actors as responding to the rationalities of a Marxist analysis of work organisation within capitalism and argues for the exploration of actors' rationalities, rather than assuming and asserting them (Salaman, 1986, p. 114).

The arguments marshalled against resurrecting the single case study as a method of researching work organisations centre on case studies not being concerned with the collection of data from samples drawn from wider populations. The issue of their (lack of) representativeness is then related to difficulties in generalising findings from just one case (Pugh, 1988; Bresnen, 1988; Dunkerley, 1988). Case study evidence has often been dismissed as idiosyncratic, since the data derived from it might be from atypical organisations. As far as this project is concerned, four points can be made in response to these criticisms of case studies.

First, the issue of the inadmissibility of generalising from one case is less pronounced in this area of work. The case study was used to test whether there was a shift in the social work labour process towards an industrial model. If this was, as its proponents claimed, a universal trend, it should have been observable in some form, and to some degree, in any Social Services Department studied.

Secondly, a Social Services Department as the site of a case study escapes the full strength of the criticism that any case which is studied is a unique context. Social Services Departments, whilst being in part the product of local political choices (see Chapter Five), have broad similarities - derived from their position as public agencies in local government with statutory duties - when compared, say, to the possibly more idiosyncratic forms of different areas of private sector activity. In other words, Social Services Departments share sufficient similarities to make a case study worthwhile, whilst still allowing for potentially interesting variations arising from their specific localities and contexts.

Thirdly, confusion arises in criticisms of case study methodology because of the assumption that any particular case studied is a sample of one. In contrast Bryman has argued that case studies should be judged in terms of theory-testing and the adequacy of the theoretical insights that they generate. The aim is not to infer the characteristics of a wider population from the findings of a case study as a sample of one, but to identify patterns and linkages of theoretical importance in the findings, which are open to replication in other cases (Bryman, 1989, pp. 172-3). 'Theoretical' case studies are conducted to be as favourable as possible to testing the adequacy of the theoretical perspective and, if necessary, modifying it (Mitchell, 1983; Yin, 1984).

Fourthly, criticisms centering on lack of representativeness and difficulty in generalisability may highlight the issue of the reliability of a particular piece of research, as conventionally understood, but neglect the issue of validity; that is the extent to which a particular research project is using a method which has validity in relation to the subject matter being studied. Giving greater emphasis to validity would mean judging methods according to the extent to which they are capable of achieving a good 'fit' between a theoretical perspective and the phenomena it purports to describe and explain. Research methods have to be in tune with the area being researched.

Having attempted to counter the criticisms customarily made of the case study approach, it is worth considering its advantages. In addition to their use in testing theory, noted above in response to the criticisms, case studies allow the researcher to place a strong emphasis on everyday activity and the context in which it takes place. Case studies can provide an understanding of organisational functioning in previously uncharted areas which are not amenable to investigation through the fleeting contact offered by, say, the quantitative questionnaire. A quantitative study is incapable of giving attention to the specific nuances of the structure of the labour process and does not provide a detailed account of how front-line managers' interpret and shape their work, the processual aspects of their role in relation to social workers and the nature of their trade union experience.

Case studies usually draw on more than one research method. The research design of this particular case study involved the use of documentary sources and semi-structured interviews. This combination of research methods was capable of eliciting structural and processual nuances and setting them in the context of the particular labour process within which they were taking place.

Documentary sources

I had unrestricted access to a huge amount of documentary data (memoranda, policy statements, procedures and the like). I was also given access to Welfareville Social Services Committee's minutes and all of Welfareville's archive material. This documentary material was used to examine the structure of the social work labour process in Welfareville; to give an historical perspective on how Welfareville's social work labour process had developed; to reveal how the structure of the labour process shaped front-line management; to outline the sort of jobs front-line managers had; and to highlight the significance of their supervision of social workers, because the material showed that Welfareville had not developed specific managerial control mechanisms. In the event, it has only been possible to bring together 'milestones' from the continuous flow of documentary data to which I was exposed. These milestones in the development of the structure of Welfareville's social work labour process, as represented by the major changes in organisation and their impact on front-line management, are presented later in the chapter.

Having access to documentary sources meant that I could collect data on matters which predated the study. The data from documents was thus capable of covering much longer time spans than would have been feasible using other approaches to data collection and key organisational changes to the labour process could be revealed.   This was a considerable advantage since, despite their notorious reputation as changeable entities, Social Services Departments are very often subjected to time-restricted, snapshot methods of research.

Interviews

A full account of the sample of front-line managers is set out in the Appendix. The sample comprised all of the front-line managers in Welfareville Social Services Department.   I regarded them as 'key informants' involved in the 'shadow structure' at the front-line level (Salaman, 1986, pp. 112-113). I wanted to interview front-line managers in order to compare their experiences of the social work labour process with the literature which addressed it, in the belief that the strengths and limitations of existing theory could be highlighted through consideration of the events and experiences of being a person in a particular context and structure.

After agreeing to take part and setting the date, each interviewee was sent a letter a week in advance listing the areas I wanted to discuss. These areas were then introduced as headings in the flow of the interview as the front-line managers elaborated on their experiences. After covering the interviewees' work history, I used the areas identified in the letter simply to ensure that everything was covered. The interviews ranged in length from one and a half to two and a half hours and were conducted immediately after the end of the working day The interviews were tape recorded.

Categorising and sorting the interview data involved the tedious slog of transcribing the tapes, reading each of the transcripts 'vertically' from start to finish several times in order to become familiar with the data, identifying the major themes having a bearing on my research interests, dividing the transcripts into sections according to those themes, reading the material 'horizontally' across the transcripts by themes, cutting up the transcripts and putting them into themed piles, juggling and sorting the material within the themes, and marking examples to be used to illustrate particular points. As no statistical significance could be attached to the results, no quantification of the data is given in Chapters Seven and Eight, apart from majority and minority views being identified where relevant, as a matter of general interest.

In setting out the combined use of documentary sources and interviews in the research, I do not mean to imply that classical 'triangulation' of data was involved. The claim made for the research methods is more modest. This combination of methods was deemed suitable for the purpose of mapping out the organisational structure of the social work labour process in Welfareville, the processes within it and the perspectives of front-line managers.

Having debated the value of the case study as an approach to the present research and set out the methods used in the case study of Welfareville, the organisational structure of the labour process in Welfareville is now elaborated.

Welfareville's labour process

The remainder of the chapter elaborates on the general representation of the levels in the social work labour process (see Chapter Five) in the local context of Welfareville's organisation of its Social Services Department. Salaman argues that work organisations represent the 'deliberate, purposive structuring of work activities and work roles' (Salaman, 1979, Ch. 1 and pp. 102-142) and as such they constitute labour processes. Clegg and Dunkerley propose 'the concept of organisation as control of the labour process' as the object of (work) organisational analysis (Clegg and Dunkerley, 1980, p. 1). Unfortunately, the early emphasis in the labour process perspective on managerial control, through scientific management techniques, led to the neglect of organisational structures as representing a range of possibilities for organising labour processes. Developments in the organisational structure of the social work labour process in Welfareville provide the framework within which the responses of front-line managers are located, both to their position in the labour process (Chapter Seven) and to trade unionism (Chapter Eight).

The remainder of the chapter is in five main sections:

- Welfareville's implementation of the Seebohm Report;
- Welfareville and the bureau-professional labour process;
- Welfareville's social work labour process;
- The labour process and front-line managers;
- Attempts at securing more managerial control.

Welfareville's implementation of the Seebohm Report

Prior to the Seebohm Report, in common with other local authorities, Welfareville Council organised its personal social services through a committee system for separate social services. There was a Children's Committee (Children's Department) and a Health and Welfare Committee (Mental Welfare Department and Welfare Department). There was no decentralisation of fieldwork services in any of the three departments. All three departments shared the same building next to Welfareville's Council House. Four of the front-line managers interviewed as part of the case study had worked in one or other of Welfareville's three pre-Seebohm Departments. Sam recalls the ethos of the centralised Children's Department:

> You knew everyone then.   If I wanted to talk to the Children's Officer it was very easy. You didn't have to plough your way through the system that there is now. You knew everybody, because it was a smaller group. Even formulating policy in the department was easy because you could all agree quickly. You could get through to the Councillors on the Children's Committee. They were familiar to us.

According to the typology developed by Payne (Payne, 1979, pp. 150-152) the type of team organisation adopted pre-Seebohm in Welfareville, as elsewhere, was that of the 'traditional team'. The organisational pattern was that of a team led by a Senior Social Worker and consisting of a group of social workers with equal status who, except for consultation/ supervision sessions, worked independently in providing individual casework. Within the boundaries of this team structure, the individual social worker had day-to-day control over her/his workload. The sense of autonomy may have been reinforced by the size of caseloads. Many social workers carried large caseloads (up to 200) which probably meant that it was difficult for their supervisors to acquaint themselves in any detail with the social worker's workload.

With the passing of the Local Authority Social Services Act (1970), Welfareville was in a position to embrace quickly the proposals of the Seebohm Report and to disband the three existing departments because Welfareville Council had anticipated the Local Authority Social Services Act becoming law on 29 May 1970. In December 1969 'Welfareville's' Policy Committee had considered a report from the Town Clerk on the implications of the Seebohm Report. Following the meeting, most of 'Welfareville's' chief officers were included in a project team under the Town Clerk's leadership to prepare a report on reorganising Welfareville's personal social services. This report went to the Policy Committee in March 1970 and the Committee approved in principle the establishment of a Social Services Committee. Welfareville was the second local authority to appoint a Director of Social Services, and the first local authority to have a Director in post on 1st September 1970. The Policy Committee, on 17 September 1970, and the full Welfareville Council, on 6 October 1970, resolved to establish a Social Services Department.   The Social Services Committee met for the first time on 20 November 1970 and the Social Services Department became operational on 1 January 1971.

Welfareville and the bureau-professional labour process

The context of Welfareville was particularly conducive to the development of the social democratic, bureau-professional model of the social work labour process contained in the Seebohm Report: a traditional Labour Council, committed to Seebohm's bureau- professional vision for social work. The ethos of Welfareville's labour process and its embodiment of bureau-professionalism is contained in an account of the first ten years of the Department, published to coincide with its tenth anniversary. The publication, which was widely distributed locally and nationally, set out a commitment to the professional standing of generic social work, regarding any problem in the professional standing of social work as stemming from the instability of its clientele:

> Social work can now claim professional status, although both its functions and methods are less well identified and documented than those of other professional activities. This is perhaps inherent to the nature of social work, which by definition is concerned with individuals in crisis, who are thereby often disorientated and confused. The contribution of social work has been to recognise the unity of approach which can facilitate solutions in serving apparently diverse and unrelated situations.

Welfareville local authority gave significant backing to its Social Services Department. Although the growth rates of 30% p.a. in expenditure in the early

1970s slowed down, expenditure had increased by £8.5 million in real terms from the establishment of the Department in 1971 until the time of the study in 1982. In the financial year 1981/2 there was a 2.9% increase in the Department's budget at a time when Welfareville Council's overall expenditure level was being reduced. This expenditure commitment by Welfareville Council to its Social Services Department is illustrated by rising staffing levels. In the period from 1972 to 1982 the total number of staff increased from 961 to 1734 and the number of field social workers   increased from 70 to 178, of whom 90% were qualified by the time of the study.

Welfareville's social work labour process

In implementing the Seebohm Report, Parsloe identifies the existence of two main patterns of organisational structure for the social work labour process: a function-based model with Assistant Directors for fieldwork services, for residential services, for domicilary and day care services, for administration and for research and development; and a geographical model, with divisional directors for all services within a specified area of the local authority (Parsloe, 1981, p. 5; and see Hallett, 1982, p. 37). Welfareville initially adopted a function-based model (see Fig. 7.1).

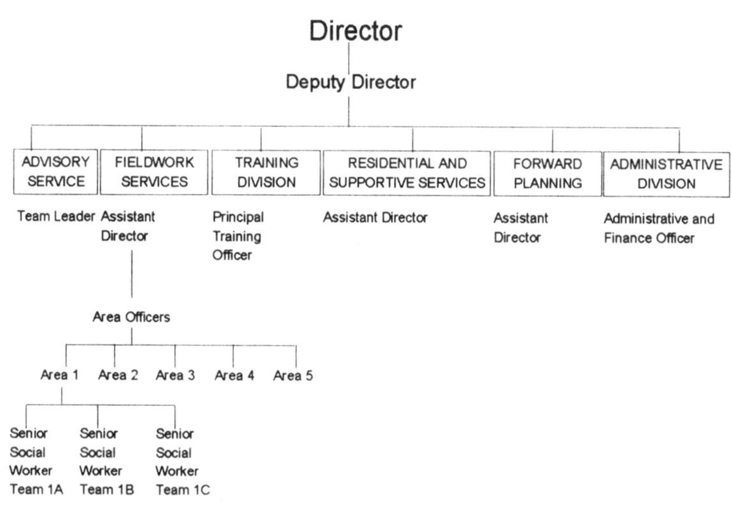

Figure 6.1   Welfareville Social Services Department, management structure 1971

Within the fieldwork division there were five middle managers, Area Officers, with responsibility for service provision for areas each with a population of approximately 60,000 people. There were three social work teams in each area. Each team consisted of a senior social worker and at least three social workers and a welfare assistant. The operational unit for the delivery of services was the area. One area office was set up in the east of Welfareville, housing all three of its teams, with the staff of the other four areas still at headquarters. In this structure the senior social workers, as team leaders, were consultants/supervisors. Grant, Irene and Tim describe the organisational structure in this period and the position of team leaders in the labour process:

[Grant] 'There were three seniors to each area so fifteen seniors had to be appointed. In each area there was an area officer, three senior social workers, and nine social workers. The senior social worker's role was supervising three people. It was literally casework supervision. We didn't even allocate cases'.

[Irene] 'Initially it was a team leader's job and the responsibilities were supervision of a small number of staff. There were no responsibilities as regards resources.'

[Tim] 'Senior social workers, after Seebohm, were not involved in policy-making. You just supervised individual staff members. It was a very circumscribed job.'

The original system of an Area Officer responsible for three teams of social workers, each with a senior social worker, was short-lived. The argument used to change this initial form of the labour process was that decentralisation to area offices was not considered to be in line with the recommendations of the Seebohm Report for more local forms of organisation. Area offices would prove inaccessible to many service users. In an interview given to the local newspaper as he left Welfareville, the Director declared that his aim 'was always to make the Department's local district offices as much a part of the street scene as fish and chip shops or banks'. Accordingly in January 1972 it was decided that area offices would be replaced by district offices covering the much smaller areas, about 20,000 population, served by the existing small teams of social workers. The decentralised district offices were still to be grouped into areas under an area officer, who would be located with one of the social work teams in one of the district offices. Then, on 2nd April 1973, the decision was taken to replace areas as the unit of operation by social work teams, now to be redesignated district teams which were to be fully decentralised over a 7-8 year period.

The district teams remained the basis for the provision of field social work up until the case study was conducted. At the time of the decision, in 1973, three of the district teams were already decentralised. By 1975 seven teams were decentralised, by 1982 fifteen teams were decentralised and by 1984 all of the, by then, sixteen teams were decentralised into the districts they served. They were based wherever premises could be found, including converted council flats, private houses, shop premises and community centres.

As we saw in Chapter Five the Seebohm Committee regarded the establishment of such locally-based area teams as a key priority. They were the cornerstone of service delivery in the Seebohm vision (Seebohm, 1968, paras 583-594) and later in the Barclay Report (Barclay, 1982). This stress on moving both the geographical site and the form of service delivery closer to the clientele affected many areas of social policy in this period and reflected attempts to make adjustments in service provision in response to the perceived failings of the social democratic welfare state. Consistent with this trend, in Welfareville decentralised teams were presented as central to the development of the Social Services Department.

In terms of Payne's typology, the social work teams in Welfareville were rapidly moving towards the transitional type (Payne, 1979, pp. 150-152). Workers were allocated to teams according to expertise, rather than according to the notion of the multi-purpose generic social worker. Home helps and occupational therapists were attached to teams for all or part of their work. Welfare assistants were appointed. Providing access to a wide range of decentralised resources through the district offices became as important as individual casework.

The labour process and front-line managers

Some of the detailed changes involved in the shift to the district team as the decentralised operational unit had a significant impact on the position of the front-line managers in the labour process. The Area Officers, who had been the outposted link between headquarters-based senior managers and the social work teams, were moved in 1975 into a centrally-based role at headquarters, and thus removed from contact with service provision. Each Area Officer was given specific co-ordinating and policy development functions, for example, in relation to hospital social work, disability services and so on. The geographical areas became administrative rather than operational units, with operational issues moved to the periphery of the Area Officer's role. Subsequent organisational changes at the middle management level consolidated these developments. In 1975 the five Area Officers were reduced to four and in 1980 they were further reduced to three and their incumbents were redesignated as Area Managers. The three Area Managers were made responsible for both field and residential services and two Deputy Area Managers with wide-ranging responsibilities worked to each of them (see Figure 7.2).

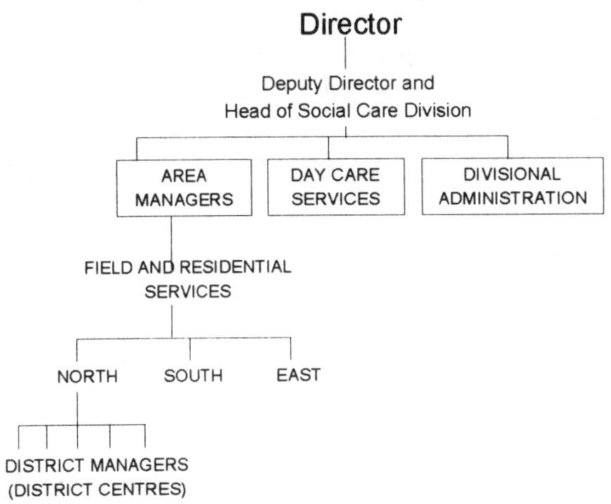

Figure 6.2   Welfareville Social Services Department, management structure 1982

Locating teams in the districts of Welfareville they served, away from the day-to-day control of Area Managers, had consequences for the position of the front-line managers in the labour process. The District Managers, as the former Senior Social Workers now became, comment on the changes in their front-line management position, produced by this geographical and hierarchical distance from their managers:

[Sam] 'We needed District Managers because social workers need somebody to refer to. You need somebody who can give a decision quickly, who can make a decision on the spot. A manager at the Council House was too remote, far too remote'.

[Ivan] 'District Managers have been given more responsibility by necessity because they are in a different geographical location than their supervising officers. That inevitably has an effect. I think they have more autonomy in the day-to-day operation of their own unit.'

The additional autonomy and responsibility which accompanied these changes in the structure of the labour process were stressed by all of the District Managers interviewed. The main shift in role was towards overall management of the team and its resources. Curtis describes his experience of this change in role, indicating that one of its implications may be a loosening, not a tightening, of control over social workers:

> The change from senior social worker to district manager is mainly a change in the areas of responsibility. Before there was an Area Officer who signed things and took decisions. You had to depend on the Area Officer for decisions about reception into care and things like that. Now, the decisions are taken here. I didn't used to have to concern myself with being responsible for petty cash and other financial things. All that has emerged very rapidly and quietly. It emerged quietly, but it combined together to put pressure on you, intolerable pressure at times. It is not a question any more of looking just at the professional side of things, it is more the heavy administration thing. There is a departmental shift to push district managers in that direction, rather than towards professional issues. They get left with the social worker.

This theme, of delegated responsibility being accompanied by a push towards overall management of a team, was mentioned by all the District Managers:

> [Malcolm] 'At that time you hadn't got any of the responsibilities you've got now. You were basically just a team leader in a small team. It was a team leader's role without management responsibility or authority. The responsibility was still with the area officer and you were responsible for the morale of your team. You did supervision. There wasn't much thinking about the deployment of resources. There wasn't much involvement in developing services to fill the gaps or responding to issues. Now you've got responsibility for budgets and the home care service.'

The emphasis on an enlarged role in relation to overall service delivery was accompanied by an emphasis on work outside the department, in the *communities* served by the district offices:

> [Tina] 'There is also all the community work you have to take part in. You have to get out and get to know who's out there and who's pulling the strings out there. All that is extra responsibility to the job'.

and on work with other *agencies*:

> [Irene] 'There is a greater expectation of district managers that they should be representatives of the department, as a manager, with other agencies. In the past the area officers were the people involved a lot more with outside agencies. We take decisions now that area officers would have taken before'.

[Sam] 'The job has changed in the sense that you've gone from just casework supervision to an almost totally managerial role. As a district manager there is all the liaison work with local doctors and so on.'

The numbers of social workers in the teams, 70 in September 1972, 178 by September 1981, and the diversity of services located in district teams by the time the research took place (Voluntary Help Organisers, Home Care Organisers, Under-Fives Services Supervisors, Hospital Social Workers, allocation of residential places), had changed the front-line manager from a senior social worker solely responsible for providing a consultation/supervision service in order to enhance the quality of casework practice, to a District Manager with added responsibilities for organisation of services, the allocation of work and external liaison. The District Managers' job description emphasised that senior managers expected front-line managers to maintain a dual emphasis on a uniform city-wide standard of services provided to individual service users and distinctive services developed in response to the needs of the district's particular community. The tenth anniversary publication, referred to earlier, emphasises the encouragement given to district teams to develop their own priorities locally 'with the obvious advantages of encouraging originality in thought and developments in practice'. The District Manager is described as the 'key operational figure at community level'.

In response to the emphasis on developing district-distinctive services, different forms of organisation had emerged in different districts even for statutory services, for example, intake/long-term splits in some District Teams, patch-based work in others. There was sufficient functional autonomy for district teams to develop theirown variants of micro-structures within the labour process at the front-line level, rather than there being a prescribed structure and modus operandi for front-line units. The corollary to this, also noted in the anniversary publication, was that the involvement of Area Officers in district teams dwindled even further and their level of the labour process shifted even more in the direction of policy co-ordination and development for specific service user groups. As a consequence, the late 1970s began to set a pattern of considerable delegation to District Managers of the responsibility for resource allocation. For example, in 1978 the Home Care Service was decentralised to district teams and chairing case conferences in residential establishments was delegated to District Managers, as was the allocation of short-stay places. The computerisation of fieldwork services in the same period resulted in district teams receiving a monthly list of open cases, a monthly spreadsheet of the total departmental caseload, and reminders when six monthly reviews were due on children in care.

The enlargement of the front-line managers' role in the labour process, the degree of autonomy given to district teams and the front-line managers' ability to control information sent through to headquarters were obstacles to control by senior management which are difficult to square with the radical social work literature's account of senior managers wresting control over the work of social workers -

unless the District Managers, as the agents of senior management, were committed unambiguously to the establishment of increasing control over social workers' practice. The data already presented throw initial doubts on such an interpretation of District Managers' position. (Their identifications and commitments in this respect are explored further in Chapter Seven.) As a senior manager himself, Bamford laments the Seebohm Committee's failure to explore the managerial implications of a decentralised structure in a large unified department (Bamford, 1982, p. 10). This failure to consider the (senior) managerial implications of decentralisation typified the approach to decentralisation in Welfareville. Welfareville's policy documents on decentralisation concentrated on the Seebohm Report's policy objectives and on practical concerns about geographical boundaries and identifying suitable office locations.

Attempts at securing more managerial control

In the mid-1970s, as the end of the early years of spectacular growth in Social Services Departments loomed and referrals continued to bombard Social Services Departments, senior managerial interest turned towards ways of rationing resources (Bamford, 1982, p. 47). Two of the techniques which were adopted elsewhere were not tried in Welfareville - caseload management (Osmond et al., 1977; Vickery, 1977) and case review systems (Goldberg and Warburton, 1979). Both of these systems of work control focused on the detailed work involved in individual cases. We are left to speculate on why no attempt was made to introduce them in Welfareville. We have already seen that Welfareville had a perception of social work as a professional activity which would have been difficult to square with detailed scrutiny of social workers' practice. In addition, after the end of the early 1970s boom, the traditional Labour Council protected Welfareville's Social Services Department by allocating slight growth from year to year, so perhaps there was less pressure on its senior managers than on those of other Social Services Departments to introduce what might have been regarded as Draconian methods of work control in the context of the autonomy established for and by district teams. The high level of union activity (see Chapter Eight), which would have been directed at preventing the implementation of such measures, cannot be discounted. However, senior managers did attempt to introduce three more general strategies for work control: an Operational Priority System, Workload Indicators and District Audits.

The purpose of *Operational Priority Systems* is to translate general policy directives into explicit priority decisions at a local level in order to ensure social workers are implementing departmental policy (Algie, 1975; Hall, 1975; Algie and Miller, 1976; Whitmore and Fuller, 1980). In 1977 the system proposed in Welfareville involved the construction of a chart with columns headed 'Primary Service', 'Minimum Service', 'Low Extension' and 'Upper Extension'. The total range of the Department's workload was broken down into a series of tasks which were fitted into one of these categories. Senior managers intended to require District Managers to stipulate the level of service being provided in the district teams for each aspect of the teams' workloads. This version of an Operational Priority System was a permissive model, as the document setting it out sought to demonstrate: 'It is felt that the determination of the minimum service level is a matter for departmental policy but that district teams should have wide discretion in deciding how they develop their services beyond the minimum service line so that they are able to provide very fine tuning to enable teams to meet the needs of their communities.'

The bureau-professional nature of the labour process in Welfareville is indicated in the accommodation made in the proposed operational priority system to professional judgement:

> Processes of selection [of priorities] involve the use of professional judgements, statistical measures and individual intuition. The tables do not replace the need for professional judgements to be made on the allocation of social work time and resources. They have been designed to provide a visible plan of services in order to clarify the levels of priority given to each aspect of generic social work being provided at the present time throughout the Department.

Permissive as this proposal was, it is the closest Welfareville Social Services Department came to the Bravermanian industrial model of the labour process represented in the radical social work literature. Even this permissive model was never implemented in the face of District Manager and trade union resistance.

Following the failure to introduce the Operational Priority System, *Workload Indicators* were developed by senior managers in order to guide the allocation of staffing resources to each district team. The work of each team was compared on a combination of population characteristics and 'work factors' for example, the number of children received into care. Each work factor was given a specific weighting and the accumulated figure which resulted was considered to correspond to the team's workload. This figure was divided by the number of social workers in the team to produce an average workload figure for each team member. It was then possible for senior managers to rate social work teams according to the workload carried by a notional team member. Senior managers were able to introduce Workload Indicators without having to negotiate agreement to the exercise as they had the information used in the exercise readily to hand. The first Workload Indicators Exercise revealed a team that was apparently over-staffed and the Indicators were used to justify a senior management proposal for transferring a social work post out of that district office. On this and on two subsequent occasions when senior managers attempted to transfer posts on the basis of Workload Indicator scores, the Shops Stewards Committee organised opposition on the basis of the allegedly crude measurements the Workload Indicators adopted which, they argued, were incapable of reflecting the subtleties of social work and were biased against preventive work. Senior managers' stance was that the Workload Indicators were only a guide, one factor amongst others which might be taken into account, for example, the degree of community involvement or the level of experience in a particular team. The senior management's proposals to transfer a member of staff were nevertheless rescinded on each occasion. The Workload Indicators Exercises became intermittent and then disappeared.

In 1981-2, an attempt was made to develop a mechanism to review the work of district teams: the ***District Audit***. District teams were to write a report covering categories drawn up by senior management. This report would be the basis for an audit of the team's work by the Area Manager which would replace the Workload Indicators. This proposal was opposed by the Shop Stewards Committee and District Managers. The first concession from senior management was that the term 'Audit' was dropped and the objectives of the redesignated District Team Reviews stressed their reciprocal nature: teams were to assess both their own performance and that of senior managers. The Reviews began and were accompanied by further lengthy negotiations for about eighteen months during 1986/7. They continued sporadically but were discontinued before all teams had been reviewed.

These three attempts by senior management to initiate systems involving an enhancement of managerial control, all foundered on the opposition of District Managers and the Shop Stewards' Committee. Both interests argued consistently and successfully for the principle of district team autonomy and the inappropriateness of 'mechanistic' methods of work control and resource allocation. Having failed to implement these managerial techniques, senior managers were left with relying on the supervision of the day-to-day work of social workers provided by District Managers (see Chapter Seven).

Conclusion

This chapter has introduced the case study of Welfareville Social Services Department and provided an account of developments in the organisational structure of Welfareville's social work labour process, up until the time of the research. In so doing, it has lent support to the bureau-professional model of the social work labour process, advanced in Chapters Four and Five, rather than the radical social work texts' industrial model, discussed in Chapter Three.

Chapters Seven and Eight consider Welfareville's front-line managers' accounts of their experiences, identifications and commitments. The material on the organisational structure of Welfareville's social work labour process, presented in this chapter, is the context in which those accounts were located and constructed.

7 Front-line managers and the management of state social work

Introduction

We saw in Chapter Six that, by the early 1980s, the front-line level   in 'Welfareville's' social work labour process was relatively autonomous, with District Managers located in decentralised district centres. This chapter explores the significance of front-line management at this level in the social work labour process through District Managers' accounts of being a manager, under the following headings:

- Learning to manage;
- Self-definition;
- Facing both ways;
- Links upwards;
- Links sideways;
- Links with social workers.

Learning to manage

All of the District Managers said that they had learned how to do their jobs primarily from an interplay of the orientation they brought to the job and their experiences gained as they went along. They did not consider that senior managers had a view of what being a District Manager entailed which was inculcated at the outset and to which District Managers had to adhere. Rather, learning to manage was achieved by muddling through:

[Tina] 'I have just learned by my mistakes. I don't think anybody is told how to be a District Manager in Welfareville'.

The lack of initial direction from senior managers was accompanied by little formal training for their role. Ten of the District Managers had had no training. The remaining four had been on a two week in-service training course with other managers from different departments in 'Welfareville' local authority. This experience was valued by all four District Managers as a time for systematic reflection on their jobs and how they might undertake them, rather than a period of socialisation into a particular 'Welfareville' view of management. They considered that earlier attendance on this course would have aided the transition to their posts:

[Jonah] 'I've learnt to be a District Manager very slowly and painfully. Eighty-five per cent has been by experience and I feel disappointed about how slow my learning has been. As a consequence of that I have made many mistakes. My first formal training as a manager took place when I had been in post three years. I went on the Welfareville Management Course. I felt quite angry then because I felt if only I had had some of that course in my first six or twelve months as a manager I wouldn't have had this or that cock-up. I just wasn't prepared for the enormous diversity of the job'.

Two of the four District Managers who had attended Welfareville's in-service management training course were also released, on separate occasions, to a nationally-based, full-time, year-long management development programme. The effect of this programme on the two District Managers concerned was very different from that of the in-service course. If the in-service course gave them an opportunity they had valued to reflect on their jobs, the management development programme disturbed their existing views of their jobs in a more fundamental sense:

[Ivan] 'I see the job differently now. Now I see the role as me helping the team to be more involved in policy and development; that it's a collective effort rather than radiating from me the ideas and the directions we should be going. When I applied for the job I thought that's the way it would be. My view of the job has changed. I don't see myself as the sole responsible person for the way the team is going. I see the job as being more about facilitating the ideas that other people have and working those to fruition. I sometimes find that a frustrating part of the job because there are things I would like to do or developments I would like to pursue and sometimes there's just not time for that or the climate's not right within the team. I think it's a case of a service being provided through other people and I see my personal influence on that as being much less than I originally thought. When I took on the job as regards the concept of a team approach my knowledge was limited. The position I've come to now, I've arrived at as a result of bitter experience and also having done the {national management development programme} and having done some reading about management. I've learnt to be a District Manager mainly through experience and going on the {national management development programme}'.

[Jonah] 'I think I've changed in terms of working with the team as a whole. Early on I had a view about control as things all passing through me, and me controlling all the knowledge in the team. Somehow controlling the debate and always being the one to read the memos and always represent the team and all the rest of it. The {national management development programme} made me realise that working in that way makes no sense at all and I learned the benefits from a much more open style. I don't now think there would be any issues which I would be unhappy to discuss in the team'.

These accounts of both District Managers jettisoning their previous ideas about management as a result of embracing an approach put forward on the management development programme they had attended, indicate the extent of strategic choice District Managers could exercise about how they defined their role in the Department from their position at the front-line level of the labour process, geographically removed from senior managers.

Self-definition

Given that for most of the District Managers there was neither formal training nor a period of socialisation from senior managers to mark their changed position in the labour process, how did District Managers define themselves?   The interviewees were invited to choose from a number of possible terms they might use to describe themselves - local government officer, manager, social worker, team leader, trade unionist and so on. In response to being asked to choose one of these terms to describe how they primarily saw themselves, eleven District Managers defined themselves as *managers* and three District Managers defined themselves as *team leaders*.

When asked about the reasons for their choices the distinctions made by the majority of District Managers (eleven), between being a team leader and a manager, did not rest on 'team leader' and 'manager' describing different approaches to their dealings with social workers. Rather the group of those who preferred the term 'manager' to describe their work stressed the responsibilities they had in addition to face-to-face work with social workers. Some of these additional responsibilities were *internal* to District Managers' work within the district centres:

[Tina] 'In the District Manager's job there's now more administration and report writing. In the past reviews on children in care and so on were chased up by an administrator.'

Having control internally over resource allocation without having to refer to more senior managers was also seen as significant:

[Curtis] 'We take decisions now that area officers would have taken before. Senior Social Workers didn't have the management of budgets. Budgets were under central control';

[Michael] 'The difference is that previously there wasn't much thinking about the deployment of your resources. That responsibility was with the area officer and you were responsible for the morale of the team. You did supervision. There wasn't much thinking about the deployment of resources. There wasn't much involvement in developing services to fill gaps or respond to issues. Now you've got responsibility for budgets and the Home Care Service. The whole atmosphere has changed. You are now seen as a manager whereas before it was a more ad hoc role. It's your responsibility and that's a management thing.'

Other responsibilities were *external* to the district centres:

[Irene] 'There is a greater expectation of district managers that they should be representatives of the Department as a manager with other agencies. In the past the area officers were involved a lot more with outside agencies'.

[Campbell] 'You've got all these agencies, Police, schools and so on and I do things with them. It all affects the way the District goes. Whatever I do is affecting what they do and thus the general running of the District'.

Although all of the District Managers, including those who chose the term 'manager' to describe their work, wanted to give a strong emphasis to their work with staff in the district centres, the three District Managers who defined themselves primarily as 'team leaders' saw their dealings with social workers in the decentralised staff group as their primary function. They stressed face-to-face work with staff in the team, above all else:

[Charles] 'I see myself as a team leader because what goes on most of the day is fairly basic support of staff at casework level. That is the one area of working on a district that you can never afford to ignore. The team very quickly begins to complain if you ignore their daily support. I see myself predominantly as that, as the team leader. That's different from a manager'.

The differences in the views of the 'managers', who stressed the assumption of responsibilities in addition to face-to-face work with team members, and 'team leaders', who emphasised the support of staff, is also reflected in their attitudes towards continued involvement in practice. The three District Managers who

defined themselves as 'team leaders' were, and thought that they should continue
to be, involved in practice:

[Grant] 'I've still got a caseload but not a large one. It's my personal preference
to continue as a practitioner and my belief that if I am to supervise staff I should
continue to develop my skills as a practitioner. I still regard that as an
important part of the District Manager's job. If I couldn't sustain my own
practice workload because of other duties I would still want to be involved as a
practitioner with other members of the team'.

[Charles] 'I've got a small caseload and I do duty from time to time. I still see
myself as doing practice. The skills we have we gather through the practice and
the practice is what it's all about. I believe that everybody should be involved in
practice.   You lose the feel of what it's like unless you are doing practice,
unless you are involved with people. I just think that I'd be hopeless in all the
other areas if I didn't have some practice. The ideal Department would have
everybody doing some practice'.

Six of the majority 'managers' group were not involved in direct practice:

[Michael] I'm not involved in practice because I'm not very good at it'.

[Sam] 'I sometimes realise how distant I am from practice when I talk to social
workers but it's important in management to stop and think. Some District
Managers are chasing their tails doing social work and just never have time to
think'.

The remaining five in the 'managers' group were still involved in practice but
wanted to leave practice behind in order to concentrate on what they regarded as
the managerial aspects of their position. To their frustration they felt either
coerced into practice because of staff vacancies or they thought that they had made
a mistake early on in how they had seen the District Manager's job:

[Brian] 'You can choose about having a caseload or not having a caseload. I
think I got it wrong personally. It does help your credibility but I can't defend
it. I think you should have credibility in your own right as a manager'.

[Jonah] 'Although I've been one of the District Managers arguing strongly that
District Managers should not carry caseloads, I do have a caseload and seem to
have quite a bit of contact with clients'.

In summary, the majority of District Managers (eleven) perceived the changes in
Welfareville's social work labour process, set out in Chapter Six, as giving them

responsibilities in addition to their duty to maintain and support team members and viewed these additional responsibilities as constituting the core of their self-definition as 'managers'. The other three had a different orientation, that of 'team leader'. They described themselves in ways which had a strong resonance with the Senior Social Worker position of Welfareville's earlier social work labour process (see Chapter Six) and were able to sustain this orientation in their position in the present labour process. Further, there were three orientations to involvement in practice: positive continued involvement; negative continued involvement; no involvement.

This ability by District Managers to exercise choice in the definitions of their jobs, and to decide whether they remained involved in practice, suggests that their position in the labour process was relatively autonomous. It appeared to be free of senior management attempts to define the front-line manager's role at this level of the labour process.

Facing both ways

The dominant theme in District Managers' descriptions of their jobs, whether they saw themselves as 'managers' or 'team leaders', was facing both ways: inwards into their teams and outwards into the rest of the Social Services Department; what Irene described as 'being Janus-faced'. They all experienced this as an uncomfortable position to be in:

> [Brian] 'The source of greatest discomfort in the job is moving from role to role, from the reception of a child into care to representing the Department in a meeting'.

> [Grant] 'The District Manager is at that bottle-neck where inevitably things get restricted. It feels as though there is pressure from both directions'.

> [Irene] 'Because I am a District Manager I straddle the fence in understanding the fieldworker aspect and the management aspect...It's not an easy thing. District Managers are in the worst possible position.'

They saw themselves as having to maintain a sense of coherence at this front-line management bottleneck:

> [Tina] 'You get a double dose. If you didn't have a District Manager the department would be like a jumper that was coming undone. The District Manager holds everything together'.

[Jonah] 'We have got all sorts of systems for communicating from the centre to the periphery and stuff comes into your in-tray all the time. It's like spokes from the centre to the rim of the wheel and the pressure goes to the rim and then it goes back to the hub again'.

Jonah sums up the consequences of facing both ways: 'I think the challenge for the District Manager is to try and make links in all sorts of directions'. District Managers' experiences of these links is the subject of the following sections.

Links upwards

As far as links 'upwards' are concerned, the District Managers identified three areas in their working relationships with more senior managers:

- representing the team's interests;
- attempting to influence policy;
- getting support for themselves.

Representing the team's interests

The District Managers all stressed the representative aspect of their work:

[Jamie] 'My primary allegiance is to the team and to the district it serves. I take as the primary role to work with the team so that it functions efficiently and delivers the most effective services to the district and to encourage the team to try and identify those unmet needs that exist on the district and to encourage the team to put forward those needs to management to gain the appropriate resources'.

[Grant] 'It's important for the District Manager to represent the views and needs of the local community and the team upwards'.

[Carlton] 'Social Workers have clear roles and Area Managers have clear roles. District Managers have a dual role of managing a particular area of the organisation but using the knowledge gained from that towards contributing to the development of services in the Department.'

However they all recognised the limitations placed on the influence they could exert in a large organisation:

[Jonah] 'Anyone who works in this job has to come to terms with the fact of operating in a hierarchical structure and it becomes more hierarchical the higher you go up in the sense not just that the pyramid is getting narrower at each stage but that the higher you go the greater the commitment to the hierarchical model. That's understandable because the further up you go the more successful the people have been in the hierarchy. It's expected of me that I will report back to the senior management about the functioning of the team and client need. The theory is that all those bits of information from District Managers will be put together by a senior manager and will make sense to the politicians. That's the theory of it. There is really too much information for the notion of feeding back to be very efficient. Given that I only manage to see the Area Manager for an hour a month, when we manage to keep the date, if I told him all the things I want him to know, it would be a fraction of 1% of what has gone on. So I don't know how management has the right information to even ask the right questions'.

[Campbell] 'I don't think I've ever got very much by going upwards and saying to the Area manager, 'my team feels this' and applying for resources with five other Districts in the Area, three other Areas in the City, fifteen other Departments in the Authority. I wonder where my influence gets lost but it does get lost'.

[Charles] 'What I understand by management is that you supervise people but that you use that information to generate new services or new strategies or approaches and I don't think unless you're particularly able or articulate that you're given very much opportunity to do that. The message I seem to get is "keep things ticking over " '.

The District Managers' sense of disappointment at the difficulties they experienced in their representation of team interests reinforced the insularity of the front-line unit in Welfareville's labour process. Their perception was that the district centre was regarded by more senior managers as the District Manager's legitimate operational arena:

[Jonah] 'I think there are limitations on what the hierarchical system can do. I can think of examples of things that have been espoused quite vehemently by Senior Managers which have got absolutely nowhere because people say they're not going to do it. Every twelve months I get sucked into the one about district centres are supposed to send in quarterly returns about use of their short-stay beds. I never have done. I've always refused to do it and everybody else refuses. I've got memos going back five years saying this must happen. That's a trivial example but there are lots of examples like that where it doesn't work. I can always say to the Area Manager that there's no way I can persuade the team to do something.'

Influencing policy

If the message District Managers perceived to be coming down from senior management when they represented their team's interests upwards was 'to keep things ticking over', how did they fare when they attempted to influence Departmental policy? The interviewees considered that the District Manager's position in the labour process was ineffectual in pursuing policy proposals unless particular District Managers had established individual spheres of influence on policy matters:

[Irene] 'As an individual you can say policy things and write things to the Area Manager and they'll be ignored, but there are a number of District Managers in this Department who are very highly thought of by Senior Management. If one of those District Managers expressed a view it would be taken account of. There are other District Managers that they dismiss. It's to do with the vehicle that you've got, in our case the Area Manager, to transmit your point of view. If you'd got Area Managers that did transmit it, District Managers would have a greater opportunity. It depends on the Area Manager whether it goes through but the personality of some individual District Managers certainly has an impact'.

[Curtis] 'Once you move outside the team it's difficult to influence things. It's part of the structure. You're totally reliant on your link person, the Area Manager, to take things on. By and large that doesn't happen in my experience. I don't think I'm influencing anything in policy terms. I don't think it's accepted in the Department that you have policy ideas of your own and that you're willing and able to present them. You become excluded from the things that you ought to be involved in'.

[Brian] 'I think individuals, if they are able and articulate, can play a significant part in the wider Department. I don't necessarily think it's to do with the formal role'.

Carlton captures some of the difficulties the District Managers experienced:

'Individual influence and pressure on policy in the organisation is rather like having a load of soldiers or starving refugees over the other side of a high brick wall who are spread out and, depending on the analogy you use, you either flip over your hand grenade or your food parcel and you lob it over the wall but you are never quite sure how things are dispersed on the other side of the wall so you never know whether what you are chucking over has any effect. It may be having a devastating or a very beneficial effect but it may be having no effect at all. Either way you don't tend to get the evidence to show what's happening. It's much more difficult trying to see what influence you are having upwards rather than downwards. I know the effect I have as a District Manager because I can see the effect on people's work and the development of services. The further up you go, power and authority is dissipated and encompasses more but when you are trying to influence upwards you are aware that there are a whole load of other people also converging on Senior Managers and it's much more of a battle and a free-for-all. That's the problem. It's hit and miss. Maybe the odd grenade lands in the right place or the odd food parcel gets to the refugee but there's a whole load of wastage.'

However, opportunism was commended as a strategy at times of senior management indecisiveness:

[Jonah] 'I'm quite pessimistic about being able to influence policy individually as a general rule but   I think there are some opportunities. Sometimes when there's consultation there's quite a lot of anxiety at the centre about what to do or say or think and if you can spot some of these conceptual vacuums you can pop your ideas in and the suggestions are taken up though working parties. It's straightforward lobbying really. What makes me pessimistic is that so often ideas are held on to tenaciously at the centre, often on very superficial evidence. I certainly see myself having a role in that and trying to make an impact on a number of things. We have always tried to respond to the annual policy review for instance.'

For the District Managers then, there was some limited potential for individuals, on the basis of having established spheres of influence, to affect policy developments, particularly if vacuums could be spotted.

Getting support

The difficulty of getting personal support from Area Managers in their supervision of District Managers was commented on by all of the sample:

[Carlton] 'There isn't any what I'd call supervision of District Managers'.

[Irene] 'I haven't had good supervision from my Area Manager. I've learned from experience. Everybody learns from experience. I've dropped some clangers'.

[Brian] 'I don't believe I've been well supervised. I have been supervised by an Area Manager who has been quite content to let me do more or less what I wanted. I didn't find that very supportive. I didn't feel challenged by it.'

By implication, there does not seem to be evidence of more senior managers being intrusive and seeking to determine the nature of work undertaken at the front-line level in the labour process.

Links sideways: the District Managers' Group

The District Managers regarded the combined influence of the grouping together of District Managers as potentially powerful in redressing some of their individual difficulties in being heard in the Department, which were discussed in the previous section. Carlton made the argument for such a grouping and, in passing, pointed to the entrenched importance attached by senior management to working through the levels in the labour process, the 'proper channels':

It's interesting that there is no official forum Welfareville-wide for the biggest group of managers responsible for such a diverse range of services which operate in the front-line. I think that's because of the organisational structure. District Managers are meant to relate to the organisational structure. It's up and down rather than across to each other. I think that District Managers have such broadly common interests that they need to have a forum. They don't react as a group in relation to major organisational change issues.

[Irene] 'I think District Managers, in terms of the wider Department, have a potential influence which they don't exercise. My own view is that District Managers could be extremely powerful if they only realised it. I think they're not due to pressure of work'.

[Jamie] 'The decision-making process in this Department really concerns me and I am not quite sure how District Managers can actually bridge that without forming their own pressure group. I fully subscribe to District Managers meeting together'.

[Charles] 'We are sixteen team leaders. The only way of us getting involved in policy issues is sixteen of us not as individuals. We are sixteen key people, key in as much as we have a knowledge of our communities which people at headquarters don't have. As individuals we have very little power but as a group we could have a fair amount of power'.

[Jonah] 'I want to get a piece of power to meet the needs of clients. I think it's important on issues to get solidarity sideways. Sometimes the power is in the team and I need the backing of the team behind me and sometimes it is in the District Managers' group'.

[Tina] 'I think the Department saw us as a threat. The Department reacted pretty quickly to us meeting {a reference to the senior management team's attempt to ban meetings of the District Managers Group}. The Department takes a defensive attitude and we've taken a defensive attitude about the things we're trying to change.'

However, the District Managers identified a number of setbacks in realising the potential power of their group, already hinted at in Carlton's comment about the 'up-down' nature of the levels in the structural organisation of the labour process. Autonomy, stemming from front-line insularity, can slip into isolation:

[Tim] 'The fact that there are sixteen district teams makes for isolation in the way that you look at the world and encourages the hierarchical approach if you are not careful. It's the team, you and the Area Manager. Being as decentralised as we are encourages tunnel vision to the centre.'

Three of the District Managers, whilst valuing with the rest of the interviewees the support to be gained from the District Managers Group, considered that District Managers' isolated positions in the labour process encouraged a competitive individualism which undermined the group's effectiveness as a vehicle for making collective representations:

[Michael] 'It's useful belonging to the District Managers' Group to share views because it can be a very isolated position. You can sometimes feel as if you are going through difficult times and it's just you. If we share those things and offer support to each other, it makes life less difficult. I'm a bit cynical about it though. Colleagues aren't as honest as they could be or should be. There is a suspicion around about what we do and how we do it. That suspicion prevents any contact or reaching out. I try and get my support from the team and not go anywhere else. You can't break down the barriers. You go to a District Managers' meeting and you come away and the reality sets in. You find out that somebody's been fiddling their statistics. You feel self-righteous because you don't fiddle statistics. You are still under pressure and not getting staff so why should they do that? Then they come along to the meeting and spout something else. That gets up my nose. If we can't be honest amongst ourselves in this organisation which puts a lot of pressure on us, then what's the point? It's difficult to put up a united front about issues because our priorities vary from District to District'.

[Brian] 'It has been difficult to get together with District Manager colleagues to talk about the job. There has been an ethos of fighting for yourself and doing the best for your District, of fighting your corner and the team expects that as well, that you fight and then come away with more than the others and it you don't it's seen as weakness.'

Links with social workers

The move to decentralised teams in the post-Seebohm period is regarded by Satyamurti as reinforcing the significance of the front-line level of the social work labour process. She sees the decentralised team as the site on which work identities were located, work was allocated, the job was learned, and supervision and peer support were received (Satyamurti, 1980, p. 44). It was at this front-line management level, often referred to in the labour process literature as the 'frontier of control' (see Chapter Two), that issues of scrutiny and control, autonomy and discretion were played out. The process of control or otherwise is made explicit at such boundaries (Hugman, 1991, p. 62), in the day-to-day operation of the labour process. Therefore, if the orthodox Bravermanian model of the social work labour process, espoused in the radical social work literature (see Chapter Three), holds any water, it is in supervision of work at the interface between management and practice that we would expect to see evidence of the imposition of external controls on social workers' autonomy and discretion. What the case study of 'Welfareville' uncovered was the absence of such controls (see Chapter Six) and the continued presence of 'supervision'.

Supervision, in the hallowed social work use of the term, is not a set of externally imposed controls. It is an indirect form of accounting for work which combines administrative, managerial, educational and supportive functions. The Seebohm Committee commended:

...the process of supervision in which a senior member of staff is responsible for assisting junior colleagues by discussion of cases and problems. Since work in the personal social services is frequently taxing and disheartening, such support and guidance is often essential...Unification, we believe, will facilitate the extension of supervision and the more effective use of those supervisory skills which are at present unevenly distributed (Seebohm, 1968, Para. 148).

Such supervision of social workers is not a means of unequivocal control, which may explain the lack of attention to it in the radical social work literature. Parsloe and Stevenson, in their study of 33 social work teams, found 'little evidence of any systematic planning by supervisors to acquaint themselves with information about all the cases being supervised by individual social workers' (Parsloe and Stevenson, 1978, p. 53). Parsloe, reviewing data from the same study, concludes that the common pattern was for social workers to decide what they wanted to talk about in their supervision sessions and that it was unusual for front-line managers to even use lists of cases as a basis for keeping a check on work being done on each case (Parsloe, 1981, p. 131). Similarly, Pithouse's study illustrates the way in which rather than being controlled by supervision, social workers controlled the agenda through carefully rehearsing their accounts of their work and not disclosing aspects of their work likely to be regarded as inappropriate by front-line managers (Pithouse, 1987, pp. 76-78).

Supervision is the key to the existence of a 'parochial professional' culture at the front-line level of the labour process. Hugman highlights the importance of Becker's work on 'profession' as a folk concept, adopted by members of an occupation, and the meanings 'profession' takes on in this context (Hugman, 1991, p. 8); in other words, seeing the world through professional eyes (Pearson, 1975, p. 22). When 'Welfareville' Social Services Department's District Managers were interviewed, they dismissed any interest in professionalism as a feature of their working lives. I asked them whether they belonged to B.A.S.W., none of them did, and offered 'professional' as one of the terms they could use to describe themselves. When no responses were elicited I thought the concept of 'professionalism' was redundant, which in a formal sense it was. At the time of the interviews I accepted their dismissiveness at face value, missing the significance of professional culture, but when I was reviewing the data from the interviews it was clear that much of District Managers' work with social workers was premised on what might be described as 'parochial professionalism', a set of values and assumptions which permeated their work as front-line managers. This parochial professionalism had nothing in common with grandiose aspirations to the professional self- determination and elitist status of, for example, medicine. It was simply a way of managing their links with social workers through attempting to construct with them a shared view of social work. Whilst supervisor and supervisee held different positions within the social work labour process, parochial professionalism was rooted in their shared occupational backgrounds. Hallet points out that in the supervisory relationship, front-line managers are also 'professionals' engaged in a process of supportive consultation about cases, without an emphasis on the status differentials between manager and managed (Hallett, 1982, pp. 52-53). Given that front-line managers were promoted on the basis of judgements made about their competence as practitioners, in supervision their seniority as a practitioner, rather than their managerial position in the labour process, was to the fore. If there was room for discussion in supervision, as a form of consultation on professional practice, there must have been areas of discretion and autonomy within which social workers operated (Hugman, 1991, p. 70) at this level in the social work labour process.

As Welfareville Social Services Department was not supplying universal provision according to well-defined and strictly applied criteria, this parochial professionalism in supervision was about developing and sharing normative

orientations to the personalised and discretionary nature of social workers'
contact with service users, rather than about the imposition of control. Satyamurti
found in her study of a London borough's Social Services Department, that
front-line managers presented a model of the supervisory relationship which
hinged on their being consultants to co-professionals. Despite these managers
being aware of wide differences among social workers with regard to their level of
experience and skills, they downplayed differences in status in supervision, even
when dealing with the least experienced (Satyamurti, 1981, p. 57). Responsibility
for sorting out work priorities rested with social workers. There might be loose
discussion of priorities in supervision sessions but these discussions did not turn
into decisions which guided social workers' actions. Social workers responded to
the pressures on them as they saw fit (Satyamurti, 1981, p. 32).

Parsloe identifies three possible functions for supervision: checking that agency
and team policies are being carried out and that work is of an adequate standard;
enriching the service to the client; assisting in the worker's professional
development. She concludes: 'In our study the last two aspects seemed to receive
more attention from supervisors than the first...on the whole, team leaders seemed
to accept personally the responsibility for staff development and to carry it out
largely in supervision sessions' (Parsloe, 1981, pp. 131-132). In the present case
study, the first function Parsloe identified, the inspectorial function, only arose
very rarely and then only if it emerged out of discussion of the other two functions.
All of the District Managers cited supervision as the way in which they attempted
to maintain the quality of the service provided by social workers to service users
from the district centres:

[Brian] 'I came to this job with a few ideas which were that people do better if
they are well supervised and supervision is the key, not management, to
improving people's work performance and job satisfaction.'

As we have seen supervision, in the social work sense, was a permissive form of
managing work which gave social workers considerable discretion over their
priorities and preferred methods of work, and over how they rationed their time
and paced their work (see Chapter Five). The evidence from Welfareville paints a
similar picture. The District Managers advocated that supervision should not be
approached on the basis of a superior-subordinate relationship in which they
prescribed and judged social workers' practice, but as a meeting of two colleagues:

[Jamie] 'I think that my management role in relation to individual team
members is to ensure a good level of functioning. I would hope that my
intervention would only be through consultation and discussion in the
supervisory process. I try to get the individual to develop professionally. I
cannot see me dropping into a situation and saying 'I'm not happy about this,

this is what I want you to do'. There is a continual dialogue on cases from which decisions come.'

In such meetings the operational autonomy of social workers was prized:

[Charles] 'I see social workers as largely autonomous. They should accept the responsibilities they have and supervision should be sharing those situations that they feel they need to talk over. If necessary, the two of us will reach some agreement about a possible course of action. I'm never sure how good I am at supervision and I find it difficult discussing situations just on the facts that you're presented with. You have to allow social workers their autonomy. It's purely intuitive'.

[Jonah] 'Supervision is about giving people a large degree of autonomy about what they do and how they get on with their work. I can't think of an example of a worker going so obviously wrong that I have had to intervene against their wishes. I start from the assumption that the worker is responsible for their caseload. I am responsible for being the best consultant I can be and being an enabler for that person. I start from the point that the worker has autonomy. I think supervision is the main way you can influence practice and I would hope that through supervision I help social workers to ask themselves the right questions in terms of interviews with clients and in carrying out decisions and making sense of them. I hope they think about whether intervention is justified at all and if so what sort and how.'

Any limitations on social workers' wide areas of discretion were seen as emanating from other levels in the labour process, as a consequence of having to function in a statutory organisation fulfilling its legislative mandate through established policies:

[Carlton] 'I want social workers to be autonomous as far as possible within the framework of the law and agency policy. One of the strong things about the autonomous and effective worker is their ability to use that combination of policy, resources and law flexibly and creatively. You can use the law and policies to put the screws back on the organisation on behalf of individual clients. It's a two-edged sword'.

[Ian] 'On decision-making in cases I am prepared to let the workers make their own decisions about clients and that they only involve me if there is something fairly crucial over the law or agency policy say in child abuse cases. It doesn't really crop up that I am the manager interfering in people's professional decision-making'.

[Grant] 'It's not my style to say I'll overrule or object to particular decisions of social workers. It's much more a case of using supervision to look at what people are doing and ways of handling cases and I only use my influence very occasionally in terms of the law or where there is clear Departmental policy. If it's something less clear-cut than that, where maybe on a professional level I'm not altogether happy about the way a social worker is handling a case, I would talk it through. I can't remember a circumstance where I have actually said "I don't agree with the way you're handling this. I don't want you to deal with it in this way". It's never come to that point. My role is largely to support what they're doing. Supervision is used differently. Some workers want to work very much on their own and make their own decisions and come to tell me what they've been doing. Others are looking for advice and guidance. I would try to influence people in supervision rather than coming the heavy and saying "that's not to be" '.

[Brian] 'You do at the end of the day have a right to intervene on some matters where it's clearly a Departmental policy rather than a technical question say about how to work with a client or something. But I can't remember ever having to tell somebody not to do something. I can't remember that happening. Most of supervision is concerned with their own developmental issues and very heavy case discussion where we're discussing what's gone on and where that leaves us. It's a very much equal discussion. It's often the worker feeling unhappy about the way a case is going and I find workers too ready to blame themselves for what's going wrong and I try to help to put that into perspective'.

[Cedric] 'I think social workers should be allowed to collect information, form opinions and reach decisions which obviously in many situations they can carry through without any interference. It would not be possible if there was a definite piece of legislation against what they wanted to do or if there was some policy within the Department. If I was a social worker I would like to think that I was the person who knew better than my supervisor what was happening in a family situation. I would be the person to say the people that had the visits. Therefore, if I am to be allowed to develop the professional way, my assessment of the situation would have to have some bearing on what's happened, so I don't interfere. I don't interfere in people's decisions because I don't find the need to. Supervision is to enable people to take decisions. I would like to think it's enabled people to get to know how each other's minds work and to know expectations about Departmental policy and statutory provisions and what good practice is about. Given that understanding, I think people should be able to function well. At this level one can help people to look at how something is presented to them and so you influence the quality of work.'

Conclusion

This chapter's consideration of the front-line level of 'Welfareville's' social work labour process has shown that the position of front-line managers was more ambiguous than the radical social work literature indicated: front-line managers neither came across as simply 'one of the workers' nor did any sense emerge of District Managers sharing global goals with senior management. They emerge as people with their own objectives and priorities who are at a 'bottleneck', facing both ways: responsible for the implementation of Departmental policy in the pursuit of the organisation's legislative mandate and, at the same time, being exposed to the day-to-day pressures on front-line social workers. The data demonstrated how District Managers accommodated these conflicting pressures. There did not appear to be much scope for bold innovative policy initiative upwards into the higher levels of the labour process. Only occasionally was a District Manager able to carry through such proposals. But there was considerable potential for day-to-day autonomy, for themselves and for their team members, given that command over local resources at their level in the labour process gave them the scope to pursue local goals.   Any limitations on social workers' wide area of discretion in the labour process did not seem to stem from senior managers attempting to control their work, or even appear to be the outcome of District Managers' own direct exercise of control, but rather emerged from District Managers' and social workers' tacit understandings as together they interpreted and implemented statutory duties and Departmental policy, generated at other levels in the labour process.   In the local labour process context, front-line managers represented themselves as guardians of the permissive, parochial-professional form of supervision in existence.

In this context, District Managers' identifications with and accommodations to trade unionism are the subject of Chapter Eight.

8 Front-line managers and trade unionism

Introduction

In the labour process perspective, trade union activity has often been seen as a barometer of managerial control. Braverman takes the view that many white-collar workers are drawn towards trade unionism because they are no longer in a position to attain membership of the professional middle class. He considers that the primary dynamic behind such unionisation was the steady erosion of the worker's autonomy in the labour process; the experience of managerial control moving the experience of white-collar employment closer to that of the manual worker:

> In such occupations, the proletarian form begins to assert itself upon the consciousness of these employees. Feeling the insecurities of their role as sellers of labour power and the frustrations of a controlled and mechanically organised workplace, they begin, despite their remaining privileges, to know those symptoms of dissociation which are popularly called 'alienation' and which the working class has lived with for so long that they have become part of its second nature (Braverman, 1974, p. 205).

In a discussion of the position of professionals located in bureaucracies, Oppenheimer sets out a similar position:

> The income position, employment picture and job condition of the increasingly bureaucratically-located professional is helping to create 'proletarian' conditions...In the process of having autonomy taken away by administrators, the professional becomes proletarianised; in defending what remains of autonomy, further proletarianisation results (Oppenheimer, 1975, pp. 224-5).

The Report of the Barclay Committee, set up by the Conservative Government to examine field social work, suggested that 'Bureaucratic development has also inevitably resulted in a division between management and worker, which provides the basis for the influence of the trade unions' (Barclay, 1982, p. 180).

As we saw in Chapter Three, this analysis of new forms of social relations at the workplace was adopted in the radical social work literature and in that literature, trade unionism as a form of resistance to managerial control was a key theme.[1] If increased managerial control was producing proletarian consciousness in the social work labour process, we might expect to uncover some of its ramifications in front-line managers' experiences in relation to trade unionism. As we saw in Chapter Three, the argument was clearly set out in the radical social work texts: field social workers were portrayed as caught up in changes to the nature of the labour process and changes in social relations at the workplace. Their trade union affiliation was depicted not just as a strategy of resistance, but also as carrying within it the seeds of a more wide-ranging politicisation.

Crompton and Jones warn against making such inferences about the socio-political attitudes of white-collar workers on the basis of their trade union membership and caution that the extent and nature of white-collar trade unionism is a complex phenomenon (Crompton and Jones, 1984, p. 167). In addition Blackburn et al. produced measures which opened to question the sort of inferences made by radical social work writers about what trade unionism represents. These measures provide an 'index of class consciousness' and assess 'the potential for class action' (Blackburn et al., 1974). Blackburn et al.'s work follows the distinction made in Lockwood's earlier writing between white-collar workers becoming involved in trade union activity and the extent to which they come to terms with its 'wider class character' (Lockwood, 1958, p. 137). Bain et al.'s review of the empirical evidence available concerning the correlation between white-collar trade union activity and the politicisation of trade union members concludes: 'The available evidence suggests that there is no simple or constant relationship between social position and either union growth or union character and that neither of these, taken singly or jointly, provides an adequate indicator of the class consciousness of members' (Bain et al., 1973, p. 109). Trade union membership and activity is, therefore, potentially problematic as an automatic indicator of political attitudes and class consciousness (Mann, 1973): 'Patterns of union membership cannot be invariably "read off" from individual places in the social division of labour in any simple fashion' (Crompton and Jones, 1984, p. 174).

In order to remedy the direct reading off by the radical social work texts of what trade unionism represents, Welfareville's front-line managers' accounts of their experiences with regard to trade unionism, linked into wider trade union developments, are considered under the following headings:

- Union activity;
- N.A.L.G.O.;
- The nature of District Managers' allegiance to trade unionism;
- The Shop Stewards Committee as workplace trade unionism;
- Trade unionism as a threat.

Union activity

All of the District Managers belonged to N.A.L.G.O. Three of them routinely attended Departmental Meetings for union members called by the shop stewards in the Social Services Department. Ten of them occasionally attended Departmental Meetings when the meetings were concerned with issues which they considered to affect directly their work as District Managers. For those radical social work writers who leaned towards an orthodox Bravermanian view of the social work labour process, this level of trade union interest amongst front-line managers would be no more than might be expected. However, in order to understand more fully the significance of what was an apparently high level of support for trade unionism amongst District Managers, we need to consider two areas: first, we need to outline the nature of the particular trade union to which these District Managers belonged; secondly, we need to explore the nature of their allegiance to that trade union.

N.A.L.G.O.

N.A.L.G.O.'s origins were as a social club and a Friendly Society.[2] N.A.L.G.O. affiliated to the T.U.C. in 1964 for tactical rather than ideological reasons (Ramsay et al., 1991, p. 43). The affiliation was justified by reference to the role of the T.U.C. in influencing government policy, rather than the desirability of making common cause with manual labour (Volker, 1966). A ballot of the membership rejected affiliation to the Labour Party in 1982, despite similar advice about the tactical and instrumental advantages of affiliation. Historically, N.A.L.G.O. did not regard itself as having major differences of interest to those of the employer. Indeed, the idea that sanctions could be taken against the employer did not surface until after the Second World War, with N.A.L.G.O. representing itself as united with the employers in the provision of a public service. This identified harmony of interests was enhanced by N.A.L.G.O.'s domination by high-ranking local government officers at national and local level, with higher grades disproportionately represented among union officers (Nicholson et al., 1981). It was the intertwining of multi-level unionism and careerism in the negotiation of standard conditions which contributed to the creation of a national local government labour market and which in the post-war period was embodied in the

Whitley Council System, set up in 1946 (Laffin and Young, 1990, pp. 17-18; Ramsay et al., 1991, p. 43). N.A.L.G.O.'s multi-level unionism manifested itself in the presence of, and the need to recruit, high-ranking staff. This multi-level unionism perpetuated a union bureaucracy which adopted 'a respectable, soft-sell approach' (Blyton and Ursell, 1982).

Two of Welfareville's District Managers convey something of the flavour of N.A.L.G.O.'s particular brand of trade unionism:

[Carlton] 'N.A.L.G.O. is too caught up in its bureaucratic machinery'.

[Campbell] 'It's as though N.A.L.G.O. is a parallel organisation to the Council. The officials are playing this game of pretending to be councillors'.

How does a consideration of the nature of N.A.L.G.O., a union with a varied membership, whose members from different levels in local government have different commitments and rationales for membership (Joyce et al., 1988, p. 132), provide us with any clues about the possible significance of trade unionism for Welfareville's front-line managers?

Crompton and Jones argue that such multi-level unionism is attractive to those in the middle of organisational hierarchies, because it can be regarded as a 'suitable compromise for their conflicting needs and loyalties' (Crompton and Jones, 1984, p. 177). A detailed research study of three Social Services Departments revealed that staff at front-line manager level saw themselves as the 'jam in the sandwich' (Black et al., 1983, p. 168) and the authors conclude that 'each sat uncomfortably at the interface between their own teams and central management' (Black et al., 1983, p. 203). We saw in Chapter Six that Welfareville's District Managers were at just such an interface in terms of their structural location in the labour process. A study of industrial supervisors illustrates the way in which multi-level unionism can appeal to staff in this position: 'It was collective strength in relation to the company, rather than against their own immediate superiors, which the union mainly offered. Indeed, many of their own managers belonged to the same white-collar union' (Child and Partridge, 1982, p. 188).

The next section considers in more detail this aspect of the appeal of multi-level unionism to Welfareville's front-line managers through an examination of the nature of their allegiance to N.A.L.G.O. The following section sets out the perceived threat to that allegiance posed by the development of workplace-based forms of trade union organisation.

The nature of district managers' allegiance to trade unionism

The nature of the trade union to which Welfareville's District Managers belonged, a multi-level union, traditionally distanced from the immediate workplace, provides a perspective on the possible significance of their allegiance to it. For the majority of these District Managers (eleven), trade union membership was not seen as an assertion of collective consciousness against the power of the employer. Rather trade unionism was considered to be important for two reasons. First, as an 'insurance policy' to be redeemed if employment or status were threatened. Secondly, to improve pay and conditions:

[Curtis] 'It should be there to support staff who get themselves into difficulties and to negotiate pay claims'.

[Tim]'There are lots of scenarios where a union and being a member of a union is both protective in terms of the broader issues of pay and conditions and in terms of the specific issues which might affect me, disciplinaries for example. Also in terms of redundancy or redeployment.'

Prandy et al. found this attitude to trade union membership to be characteristic of public sector employees: 'Unionateness does not vary to any great extent by hierarchical position and associated rewards.   Much more than in private employment it is seen at all levels as an appropriate response to a situation of dissatisfaction with income' (Prandy et al., 1982, p. 164). In another study of a local authority, Crompton and Jones reach similar conclusions concerning higher rates of union membership in supervisory positions than in the lower grades (Crompton and Jones, 1984, p. 202). The attitudes of the District Managers towards trade union membership can, therefore, be regarded as part of a more widespread phenomenon in the public sector.

This widespread phenomenon took a particular form in Welfareville. In many local authorities trade union membership was part of the organisational culture. In Welfareville, this was true to such an extent that the District Managers had not had to make a conscious decision to join N.A.L.G.O. They had joined at the instigation of Welfareville Social Services Department's Personnel Section. When starting work in Welfareville union membership was offered, and the membership form signed, along with sorting out entry into the superannuation scheme and other 'first day at work' matters. New starters had to consciously opt out of union membership by being sufficiently discriminating to isolate trade union membership from all of the other routine form-filling on the first day in the job. Nevertheless, having joined, Welfareville's District Managers did not seem in any haste to leave. How are we to account for this?

Mention has already been made of the appeal of the union to District Managers in terms of an 'insurance policy'; negotiating pay and conditions and representing its members on an individual basis. In addition, as the Appendix shows, many of the District Managers expressed strong motivation to succeed in their individual careers. Distanced multi-level trade unionism was compatible with maintaining their status and ensuring that they continued to be recompensed in line with that status. Thus, collective representation in relation to pay and conditions at the national level was seen as legitimate. Collective action was not:

> [Jamie] 'I don't think trade unions realise the conflict that they can create in people when they ask for militant action. I would not strike under any circumstances.'

Indeed, far from implying the dawning of proletarian consciousness, as depicted in the radical social work literature, front-line managers might have joined N.A.L.G.O., (or, more accurately in Welfareville, not left N.A.L.G.O.), 'not because they rejected their middle class aspirations but because they see unionism as a better way of obtaining them' (Strauss, 1983, p. 204).

The advantages to District Managers of this form of trade union membership were given added bite by the threats they faced during the early 1980s. The general atmosphere of public expenditure cuts since the mid-1970s (and the consequent decline in real incomes), cash limits, incomes policies and the curtailment of career opportunities was fertile ground for the development of this form of trade unionism:

> It is the welfare professions above all that have suffered from the sudden contraction of those prospects and conditions normally thought to give them the edge over even the best paid manual workers. The fact that the semi-professions are heavily concentrated in the public sector, producing non-marketable goods, renders them especially vulnerable to those solutions to the fiscal crisis of the state that seek to divert resources into the manufacturing and productive sectors...What is new is the unexpected deterioration in conditions of work and life-chances following hard on a period of comparative munificence (Prandy et al., 1982, p. 163).

In Welfareville we have seen that the Social Services Department was afforded some protection at times of cuts in other Department's budgets (see Chapter Seven). Nevertheless, in Welfareville, and nationally, the removal of opportunities for individual advancement, previously offered by progression through bars and merit increments, was symptomatic of the changed situation in which District Managers found themselves with regard to personal advancement. Despite these circumstances, and Welfareville's District Managers' support for trade unionism possibly as an adaptation to them, this group of managers wanted to retain a dividing line between what they saw as trade union issues and professional issues:

> [Grant] 'I feel that the union has its most important part to play in terms of looking at terms and conditions of service. Their primary function is the protection and improvement in conditions. I'm much less happy when they

move into areas to do with professional decision-making. They are on a much less sound knowledge base and I worry about the appropriateness of that.'

In fact, when this opposition to trade union involvement in 'professional' issues was carefully explored, it was revealed as opposition to workplace forms of trade union activity which questioned the existing mechanisms within which parochial professional discourse took place (see Chapter Seven):

[Michael] 'One of the things that concerns me about the union is the way that particular issues are approached. What seems to happen is that the trade union is used to represent people's views on professional issues, when ordinary departmental channels for representing views and putting forward opinions haven't been used fully. On the child care policy package there is the union concern to pursue the conditions of service of particular members, which is its proper job, and making representations about broader professional issues. The two seem to get mixed up. It seems a pity if it's only through the union that people can make their views heard in the Department. It seems as though that's happened because it's seen as a more effective channel of communication. It's as though there's an attempt to turn it into a professional body, rather than sticking to conditions of service.'

The 'child care policy package' referred to here was used frequently by District Managers as a then current illustrative example of the union overstepping the mark in developing alternative policy proposals to those of senior management, in this case for the reorganisation of Welfareville's child care services. When the District Managers voiced their doubts about the trade union's involvement in issues such as the reshaping of child care services, their opposition was directed not towards the distanced multi-level union which attracted their allegiance but towards the activities of the Social Services Department's N.A.L.G.O. Shop Stewards' Committee. This form of trade unionism drew out marked differences of attitude amongst the District Managers, in contrast to their unanimous support for traditional multi-level trade unionism.

The shop stewards committee as workplace trade unionism

The 1970s witnessed the rapid growth of the shop stewards committee as a form of trade union organisation in Social Services Departments and elswhere in local government (Nicholson et al., 1981). The development of shop stewards committees received official approval in 1976 when N.A.L.G.O. both supported and issued advice on the introduction of shop steward systems with the shop steward depicted, amongst other things, as a negotiator, a role previously reserved for branch officers (N.A.L.G.O., 1976; Joyce et al., 1988, p.2). In Welfareville an ad hoc Fieldworkers' Group was formed in 1974, which sought to participate in direct negotiation with management over policy issues and departmental decision-making. In 1976 this group was reconstituted as a Shop Stewards' Committee within NALGO and shortly afterwards the local NALGO branch adopted a shop steward system throughout the local authority.

The shop stewards committees aimed to involve rank and file members at the workplace - 'to build up trade union consciousness within [the shop steward's] own section' (Brake and Bailey, 1980, p. 19) - and thus to develop a more activist, militant trade union stance in social work than that which had been traditionally associated with N.A.L.G.O. (CaseCon, 1975; Satyamurti, 1980, p. 197; Simpkin, 1983, pp. 144-148; Joyce et al., 1988, pp. 8, 37, 41). The rank and file stance advocated was premised on a view of N.A.L.G.O. as an authoritarian union with a leadership consisting of a privileged and conservative stratum of bureaucrats who collaborated with the employers against the interests of union members (Joyce et al., 1988, p. 243). In their stead, largely autonomous shop stewards would act as grass roots leaders initiating direct action (Joyce et al., 1988, p. 256). The goals of this greater degree of militancy were not just to improve the conditions of Social Services Department employees but also to improve the lot of service users (Bailey and Brake, 1975, pp. 19-20; Cockburn, 1977, pp. 168, 175; Corrigan and Leonard, 1978, p. 21). This involved developing 'an alternative network to that of management' (Garrett, 1980, p. 201) which challenged both managerial power and the hold of multi-level, bureaucratic trade unionism. This form of union organisation involved not only challenging management policies and management's right to manage (Davey, 1977; Satyamurti, 1980, pp. 40-42; Leeds S.W.A.G., 1983) but also was portrayed as an arena for class struggle (Corrigan and Leonard, 1978, pp. 143-147), particularly as the social work strikes of 1978-9 developed (Bolger et al., 1981, pp. 68-77).

The extent to which the shop stewards committees realised the ambitions of this rhetoric is, of course, a matter for debate. What was significant in terms of the attitudes of Welfareville's District Managers to trade unionism was that the oppositional stance adopted by the shop stewards movement invoked the District Managers' hostility, even though, at a general level, they recognised the need for representation. What they wanted from their union was a professionally-run negotiating service:

> [Brian] The union ought to have qualified people, not just a colleague from down the road who might think "Oh God!, this could be me next time!" I'd rather see people from outside the Department as the union person. Proper union officials.'

If District Managers' experience of work was substantially determined by increasing senior management control over the front-line level of the social work labour process, their proletarianisation driving them into common cause with field social workers, we would have expected a high level of identification on their part with the shop stewards' movement. But, as we have seen, the District Managers were committed to what Mercer and Weir call 'limited instrumentalism' which involves 'assent not to the values...but to the possible efficacy of trade unions in obtaining tangible benefits for their members' (Mercer and Weir, 1972, p. 57). This attachment to a unionism with limited instrumental goals, to, in Prandy et al.'s terms, 'enterprise unionateness' (Prandy et al., 1982, Ch. 6) was, as we have seen, compatible with District Managers' individual aspirations at a general level and preserved the common ground of parochial professionalism with social workers (see Chapter Seven).

District Managers' organisational location in the labour process, symbolised historically by the shift from Senior Social Worker to District Manager (see Chapter Six), placed the District Managers in a position of 'high trust', in relation to Senior Management, for the operation of district teams:

[Charles] 'My commitment and responsibility is to the Department. I do identify who my supervisors are and that there are certain expectations on me to do certain things and manage the team. I take that as the primary role. To manage the team so that it functions efficiently and delivers the most effective services to the district.'

In addition, District Managers held a position of greater privilege than field social workers in relation to their contact with senior management. Carter argues that such 'high trust' jobs which provide a degree of individual control and initiative in relation to job performance substantially restrict the perceived need for collective representation on job control issues and increase the emphasis on pay as the main object of collective organisation: 'Middle class labour performs high trust jobs and its trade unionism as a consequence has less concern with issues of control of working methods because these are less often under attack' (Carter, 1979, pp. 313-314).

The position of District Managers in the labour process will, therefore, clearly affect their attitudes to workplace trade unionism but does it determine them or are District Managers able to emphasise selectively certain aspects of their position in the labour process?

Three of the District Managers, whilst supporting the claims of a multi-level trade union to protect and improve individuals' pay and conditions, also supported the development of the local Shop Stewards Committee and the workplace-based form of union organisation it had instituted. They considered it was important to have a balance of power within the Social Services Department:

[Ivan] 'I think the influence of the Shop Stewards Committee has been a positive one. In general, the trend is not one that I would wish to see reversed. I don't support the view that the union has too much power. In fact, I think workers and clients have failed to look at some of the common ground between them, in terms of taking action'.

[Carlton] 'It's difficult as a District Manager negotiating the boundary between the organisation's needs and workers' needs. The boundaries between what workers want and the organisation wants is a very difficult issue. It's a very sensitive triumvirate: the workers, the union and management. I see it in terms of countervailing power. There are institutional mechanisms negotiating the balance of power'.

[Jonah] 'My view is that the Shop Stewards Committee is necessary and that it's right that people have that sort of organisation available to them, particularly when the chips are down for example   over the child care policy issues. If there hadn't been an organisation set up to make a response from the trade union point of view, there would have been little chance of altering the steamroller that was going. I said at the time, however much the District Managers might protest about it, unless there was a way of conveying to Senior Management that these proposals were opposed by a considerable number of staff, then that point of view would not be listened to. So I see it as a necessary balance to the power that employers and managers have.'

Although these three District Managers were not advocating a usurpationary strategy for the Shop Stewards Committee in relation to senior management, they had quite distinct views when compared to the majority of District Managers. They saw workplace trade union attempts to change management decisions as having a legitimate role in the development of departmental policy. Did these three District Managers have anything in common with each other, which they did not share with the others?

  All three were men from manual working class backgrounds. Although in such a small sample this is obviously not   significant, it does mirror the findings of Prandy et al.: 'The sons of manual workers are more unionate, and so are those whose fathers were themselves members of a union. This is even more true of employees in the public sector' (Prandy et al., 1982, pp. 163-164). All three had previous experience as shop stewards. In addition, one had been the Secretary of Welfareville's Shop Stewards Committee and one had unionised a voluntary agency in a previous post. These data allow us to suggest that the majority's preference for the 'limited instrumentalism' of the distanced multi-level union and this minority's additional support for workplace unionism is not determined by District Managers' position in the labour process. This accords with Nicholson et al..'s finding that support for participation in union activities is 'firmly identified as less in the sphere of work experience than in more widely based value orientations' (Nicholson et al., 1982, p. 212). The three District Managers were not supporting workplace unionism as a protest about their position in the labour process - all three were highly committed to their present posts and future careers - but rather were bringing their values and commitments into their work. In addition to their working class backgrounds, 'educated radicalism' external to the workplace appeared to be significant. All three District Managers were graduates and described becoming 'politicised' as undergraduates.

It seems then that the ideological commitments of these three to trade unionism were being carried over into their work as District Managers. Two of the three District Managers mentioned 'ideological commitment to trade unionism' in those very words. The other, his 'recommitment to strong trade union organisation'. However, we should also note that these three District Managers' ideological commitments appeared to be shaped by their present position in the labour process into a form of corporatism - they stressed the 'balance of power within the Department' and 'countervailing power' - rather than the solidaristic collectivism prized by the radical social work texts. Perhaps the 'balance' provided by trade unionism in this corporatist view allowed them to regard their prior ideological commitments as valid, but from their present position in the labour process they embraced a different view of the Department's organisational structure and operations which also led them to identify to some extent with the problems of senior managers.

Trade unionism as a threat?

The situation of District Managers as both trade union members and front-line managers raises, as we have seen, the issues of the nature of their allegiance to the trade union and how that allegiance is 'squared' with their position in the labour process. However, for District Managers trade unionism also emerged in another guise: the union presence in the front-line units - the decentralised district centres - in which they worked. In the workplace they experienced trade unionism not just in relation to the demands it made on them as union members but also in their position as front-line managers. As we saw earlier, it was precisely this form of workplace trade union organisation which the majority (eleven) of the District Managers questioned and from which they wished to distance themselves.

First, we will examine the approach to the union in the workplace taken by the three District Managers who supported the development of workplace trade unionism. Two of these three District Managers, consistent with their view of workplace trade unionism as a countervailing power in the wider Department, considered that the union was necessary in order to perform a similar function of achieving a balance of power within the workplace. They saw the union as having a clear, separate identity and power base. As such, they had received its support, as union members, and they had come into conflict with it as front-line managers. The District Manager who earlier in this chapter had spoken of the need for union/service user alliances had 'had times as a manager here when I have come into conflict with the union line' [Ivan]. The District Manager who earlier had referred to the 'very sensitive triumvirate - the workers, the union and management', described graphically how he experienced his position in this triumvirate as an issue was played out concerning cuts in staffing:

[Carlton] 'It is a fact of life that all organisations must adapt to change whether that is an increase in resources or a decrease in resources. To strike the balance for a manager between the necessity of organisational change and adaptation, on the one hand, and selling out to one's personal principles, and the sympathies that one has with the workers and the union on the other, is a very difficult dividing line to draw. Inevitably, one is compromised but it's a question of keeping a balance between the two and setting up bridgeheads for conflict resolution. I think it is naive to expect the manager to be able to do it single-handed. I see it in terms of countervailing power. I also see it in terms of democracy, otherwise unions would be outlawed. There are institutional mechanisms negotiating the balance of power. For instance, the team refused to take on work associated with posts which had been cut. There was a crisis between the organisation's need to get that work done and the families' needs to be helped and the workers' resistance to taking on the work. I talked to senior management about taking the dispute outside the team. Senior management were saying you get that work done and if you can't, you do the work. I refused to do the work and I was threatened with a disciplinary as a manager. It was taken out of the team by shop stewards and was satisfactorily negotiated by shop stewards and senior management. Those cases were allocated in a part of the team where there was actually a lot of spare capacity. Overall, one can take a balanced view but at certain stages one can be in a very unbalanced position, so throughout that issue I was discussing the question of allocation with the team, pointing out the need, pointing out that it was statutory work. With the Area Manager I was saying there is going to be conflict, we need to negotiate with the union, and in fact it was only for a brief period that my personal position was out of balance. A period of four days. Things came to a head. It didn't change my view of how it should be handled but my personal position changed. My overall strategy was uniform and consistent but I was the victim of certain pressures which I couldn't hold back, so for four days I was in an invidious position.'

For the third District Manager, this approach - 'sitting on the fence' as he called it - to the dilemmas raised by workplace trade unionism was no longer satisfactory. He supported the union 'line'. In other words, the allegiance to the trade union presence in the team was no different to wider trade union solidarity and when trade union action was necessary, managerial authority had to be laid aside:

[Jonah] 'We had an issue here about unallocated cases and I think I sat on the fence over that, seeing management's point of view and the union's point of view. It took me some time to think over the issues of where I did stand. I thought I had got to have some loyalty to management and some loyalty to the team. In fact, I got the worst of both worlds because I was seen as not being particularly loyal to either side. I realised afterwards that I hadn't clearly worked out my own views about whether it was right to say that we are going to leave so many cases unallocated if you freeze this post. I came to the conclusion that yes it was right that some sort of stand had to be made and O.K. it was unpalatable in some respects for clients not to receive a service, but there has to be some recognition at some point that if you reduce resources you have to reduce the service you provide, and that's where the N.A.L.G.O. Shop Stewards Committee comes in.'

For the other eleven District Managers, the presence of non-union workers was valued, as was the District Managers' ability to tolerate the union presence, making pragmatic decisions on how it should be handled:

[Tim] 'I have got a team which is 50/50 union and non-union members. At the time of a walkout, half the team was at work'.

[Jamie] 'It's my job to ensure that the trade union representative gets a reasonable amount of freedom and the team knows what's going on. It's also important that I get information to staff about any disputes.'

Given the general views expressed earlier by the majority of District Managers, the tolerance they expressed towards trade unionism at the workplace is surprising. How are we to account for the divergence between their reported actions and their stated views?
The potential for the structural isolation of the District Manager in Welfareville's labour process (see Chapter Six) and the difficulty of sustaining contact with other District Managers (see Chapter Six), may suggest that front-line managers were impelled towards social workers as a source of day-to-day social support (Satyamurti, 1980, p. 44). This presumably accounts for the findings in a study of social services teams, that although centre-periphery communication rests on front-line managers, implementing senior management policy was considered by front-line managers to be a small part of their role (Parsloe and Stevenson, 1978, p. 53). Parsloe also notes the reluctance of front-line managers to use the level of authority invested in their formal role and the group pressure created by union membership in the 'close atmosphere of teams' (Parsloe, 1981, p. 76).
Perhaps this explains why, whatever they say their views are about workplace unionism in the privacy of a research interview, in terms of their accounts of managing their position in the social work labour process, the majority of District

Managers considered that forcible opposition to the union presence would have set up a barrier of authority relations which would have made it difficult, if not impossible, for them to operate in the team, given the parochial-professional basis of the working relationships needed to sustain the labour process (see Chapter Six). Their approach to the union presence in their teams could not be allowed to jeopardise social workers' continued co-operation in the labour process. Their antagonism in terms of general principle had to remain muted and sit side-by-side with continuing day-to-day co-operation with trade unionism.

Conclusion

Welfareville Social Services Department's front-line managers appeared to have retained their allegiance to multi-level trade unionism in response to specific pressures and in line with individual aspirations. In addition, three District Managers, with prior ideological commitments, made sense of trade unionism in different ways to the majority in terms of the need to check the unbridled power of management and, for one District Manager, in terms of the rediscovery of a sense of union solidarity. For the majority of Welfareville's District Managers, trade union membership was accepted as a self-evident fact of working life. Their commitment to distanced multi-level unionism had not 'radicalised' them towards a general commitment to collective organisation as a means of opposing senior managers over day-to-day work issues or overall policy. They displayed a pragmatic combination of commitment to collective representation, (when they judged it necessary either for their own protection, or for their own advancement, or in order to operate in the workplace), and a continuation of their individual career aspirations. Thus, a commitment to trade unionism by District Managers, aimed at ensuring they received what they considered themselves to be worth, was not incompatible with a desire for promotion. For the majority of District Managers, the nature of their union commitment flies in the face of the radical social work literature in not constituting commitment to a union movement seeking to change Departmental policy, let alone the existing capitalist order.

In the radical social work texts, trade union developments within social work in this period were understood through a model supplied by traditional (male, manufacturing) unionism. The specific context of social work trade unionism - a bureau-professional labour process with a parochial-professional culture at the front-line level (see Chapters Five and Six) - was ignored. In the radical social work literature this led to the neglect of two issues.

First, the ways in which forms of trade union commitment and activity are adapted to specific forms of labour process, in this case a bureau-professional labour process shaped in a period when social democracy held sway in the public sector. Secondly, the influence of specific local conditions on trade unionism (Joyce et al., 1988, p. 136). The data highlights the significance of these two issues. Given the split over the desirability of workplace-based unionism between the majority/minority groups within Welfareville's front-line managers, it is difficult to support the radical social work writers' view that changes in the labour process were leading to a congruence in responses to trade unionism as a form of resistance to increasing managerial control. For both majority and minority groups, their identifications with trade unionism appeared to have been shaped by experiences and ideological commitments which they brought into their work as District Managers.

This emphasis on the experience of work as marginal in its effect on the precise nature of trade union activity has led to the development of a 'rational choice' model of trade union allegiance. Crouch argues that trade union behaviour 'can be seen as the outcome of rational choices by actors who have calculated how best to maximise their interests, given the constraints of their situation' (Crouch, 1982, p. 76). Thus, those with the most to preserve are more likely to belong to trade unions. Nevertheless, it is significant that given 'the constraints of their situation' it is to trade unions that District Managers turn. Different District Managers may interpret their allegiance to unionism in different ways but the context of their interpretations, and the constraints of that context, push them towards trade unions rather than other responses. It may not be class consciousness, but it may be indicative of the shifts in their position, a response to the growing uncertainties in their employment referred to earlier. Their reasons for belonging to a union were very different from what they would have been, say, fifteen years previously. Then it would have been impossible to conduct interviews which covered similar ground. At the very least, their allegiance to trade unionism indicated a basic consciousness of some common interests with other employees and that those interests are not always identical with those of the employer.

Perhaps the data shed some light on the work orientations versus labour process debate which has taken place. Many studies have followed Goldthorpe et al. in giving primacy to orientations to work rather than experience at work in generating particular states of trade union consciousness (Goldthorpe et al., 1968; Brown, 1992, Ch. 4). The argument advanced here is rather different to this 'work orientations' thesis. It is essentially that the experience of work does appear to shape consciousness in a general sense - for instance, none of the District Managers wished to abandon trade union membership - but that District Managers' position in the labour process does not determine the nature of their identification with, and degree of commitment to, trade unionism. An exclusive emphasis on orientations would have wrenched District Managers from the real life world of work, of public expenditure cuts and vacant posts. An exclusive emphasis on the labour process would have led us to expect District Managers either to have been made more class conscious by the universal trend towards proletarianisation or "bought off" from any commitment to trade unionism by their position of high trust in the labour process. But, they are neither automatically radicalised by the labour process nor de-unionised because of the degree of managerial authority they hold. The data do not, therefore, support either the work orientations thesis or the orthodox Bravermanian model of the radical social work literature. The District Managers were not using the union to struggle over job content, nor to express dissatisfaction with senior management by unambiguously throwing in their lot with social workers.

Notes

1 In the radical social work texts, there was a debate about the form trade union activity should take. Corrigan and Leonard were optimistic about the use to which existing trade union structures could be put (Corrigan and Leonard, 1978, p. 156). Jones (1983, pp. 139-140, 144) Simpkin (1983, pp. 145, 157) and CaseCon (1975, pp. 146-147), on the other hand, advocated reliance on the construction of rank and file organisations. Despite this debate, shop stewards committees, of the type described by Simpkin, won universal approval in the radical literature: 'The best union organisation so far suggested for social services workers is based upon the recognition of work sites as the basic unit, each with its own shop steward elected from the membership. Depending on the size of the department these stewards should form a committee or committees with direct negotiating rights with management' (Simpkin, 1983, p. 147).

2 For histories of N.A.L.G.O., see Lockwood, 1958; Spoor, 1967; Maybin, 1980.

9 Conclusion

Past patterns

After a presentation of Braverman's work on the labour process (see Chapter Two), which portrayed scientific management as the pervasive driving force for control in the monopoly capitalist era, the most pertinent aspects of the post-Braverman debate were reviewed using four key themes: managerial control strategies; the indeterminacy of labour power; worker consent; and monolithic management. Work within the labour process perspective which addressed these four themes was regarded as having combined to undermine the determinism of Braverman's original model of the labour process. Such work established first, that a variety of managerial control strategies existed; secondly, that the processes involved in transforming labour power into actual labour are not straightforward, particularly given the existence of worker resistance; thirdly, that the possibility of worker consent has to be considered as an alternative to the imposition of managerial control; and fourthly, that management is not necessarily a monolithic interest. Evidence from the studies reviewed in Chapter Two suggested the existence of diversity in labour processes, rather than the crushing uniformity presented in the work of Braverman and early labour process perspective writers. The evidence also undermined the case made by later writers who sought for an alternative ultimate logic towards specific means of control with which to replace the toppling of Braverman's reliance on scientific management. Allowance for the existence of labour process diversity pointed to the need to provide accounts of the way in which work is organised in specific circumstances and why particular forms of work organisation are found. It opened up for consideration paid work of all kinds, in place of the labour process perspective's early preoccupation with manual industrial labour. It was then argued that the literature review of the labour process perspective suggested two bearings which might guide the study of labour processes in specific contexts: first, their heterogeneity and secondly, the need for approaches which combined an analysis of the organisational structure of a labour process with the work processes through which that structure functions.

In the orthodox Bravermanian approach to the labour process which was adopted in the radical social work literature (see Chapter Three), the social work labour process was represented as having moved, and as moving still further, towards an industrial model which had steadily encroached on the autonomy of front-line field social workers through managers' wresting of control over their work. In the radical texts these developments were depicted as part of the universal trend towards managerial control in the monopoly capitalist era, as set out by Braverman. The radical social work arguments were evaluated, first, against the four key themes identified in Chapter Two's discussion of the development of the labour process perspective and secondly, against the type of approach to the study of the structure and process of specific labour processes which Chapter Two had advocated. The evaluation of the radical social work model of the labour process raised questions in relation to four issues: first, the extent to which managerial techniques of control had been, and were being, introduced; secondly, the emphasis on collective oppositional strategies to the neglect of the possibility of worker consent; thirdly, the assumption of the existence of a monolithic management interest; and fourthly, the significance of front-line managers' position in the social work labour process, not least in relation to the first three points. The accumulated weight of questions raised in relation to these four issues suggested that the radical social work paradigm's use of an orthodox Bravermanian model of the social work labour process, rooted in an assumption of common structural developments across a wide range of labour processes, failed to explore the social work labour process's distinctiveness. It was argued that in order to further understanding of the social work labour process the interdependence of structure and process needed to be studied.

An alternative model of the social work labour process to that of the industrial model employed within the radical social work paradigm was presented (see Chapter Four). Consideration was given to the directions in which the labour process perspective needed to be developed in order to take account of the social work labour process's distinctive features. The social work labour process was located within the political relations of the state as a basis for elaborating the distinctiveness of state-mediated professional work in general and the bureau-professional form of the social work labour process in particular. The consolidation of the bureau-professional social work labour process, through the implementation of the Seebohm Report in the context of the social democratic welfare state, was explored and the bureau-professional social work labour process was elaborated as being stratified on a number of relatively autonomous levels (see Chapter Five).

The case study of Welfareville Social Services Department was introduced and data from the case study were presented (see Chapters Six to Eight) in order to test the bureau-professional model of the social work labour process, (developed in

Chapters Four and Five), against the industrial model from the radical social work paradigm (presented in Chapter Three). Developments in the organisational structure of the specific social work labour process of Welfareville Social Services Department, following the implementation of the Local Authority Social Services Act (1970), were set out (see Chapter Six). The relative autonomy at the level of the front-line unit in 'Welfareville's' social work labour process, with District Managers located in decentralised district centres, was noted as the context within which front-line managers worked. The position of District Managers in the labour process at the front-line management level was then considered through front-line managers' accounts of their identifications and commitments in relation to management (see Chapter Seven) and trade unionism (see Chapter Eight).

 In Welfareville the position of front-line managers in the labour process was more ambiguous than the radical social work literature suggested (see Chapter Seven). The District Managers did not share global goals with senior management, nor were their interests merged straightforwardly with those of social workers.   They emerged as people with their own objectives and priorities at a 'bottleneck', facing both ways: responsible for the implementation of Departmental policy in the pursuit of the organisation's legislative mandate and, at the same time, being exposed to the day-to-day pressures on front-line social workers. The data demonstrated how District Managers accommodated these conflicting pressures and the considerable potential for day-to-day autonomy, for themselves and for other team members, given their command over resources at the local level in the labour process. Any limitations on social workers' wide area of discretion in the labour process did not seem to stem from senior managers attempting to control their work, through District managers being used as agents of senior management, nor did it appear to be the outcome of District Managers' own determination to exercise control. Rather it emerged from the District Manager and social worker together interpreting and implementing law and agency policy, generated at other levels in the labour process, through the parochial-professional mechanism of supervision.

Welfareville's front-line managers were shown to have retained their allegiance to multi-level trade unionism (see Chapter Eight) in response to specific pressures and in line with individual aspirations. Three District Managers also had prior ideological commitments to trade unionism. For the majority of Welfareville's District Managers, their commitment to distanced multi-level unionism had not 'radicalised' them in the direction of a general commitment to collective organisation and activism as a means of opposition to senior managers over day-to-day work issues or overall policy.   The nature of their union commitment flew in the face of the arguments in the radical social work literature that changes in the labour process were leading to a congruence in responses to trade unionism as a form of resistance to increasing managerial control. Two important aspects of trade union activity emerged: first, the significance of the ways in which forms of trade union commitment and activity are adapted to specific forms of labour process, in this case a bureau-professional labour process constructed in a period when social democracy held sway in the public sector; secondly, the importance of specifically local conditions in influencing the nature of trade unionism. These two aspects appeared to have shaped front-line managers' trade union consciousness in a general sense, but did not appear to have determined the precise nature of District Managers' identifications with trade unionism from their position in the labour process.

Future prospects

Since the data leading to these conclusions was gathered in the early 1980s, the context within which social work operates has changed fundamentally (Langan and Lee, 1989, pp. 2-3; Jones and Novak, 1994), with bureau- professionalism having been identified by the New Right as a barrier to the reconstruction of the state and its role in welfare (Clarke et al., 1994, p. 3; Clarke and Newman, 1993, pp. 48-49; Newman and Clarke, 1994, p. 23) and management occupying an increasingly significant role in the reorganisation of the welfare state (Pollitt, 1990; Clarke et al., 1994; Newman and Clarke, 1997).

The implications of material derived from a consideration of the state social work labour process in the early 1980s for this changed context in which social work finds itself are explored in relation to four areas:

- Managerial strategies;
- Levels in the labour process;
- The social work labour process and the service user;
- The labour process perspective and social divisions.

Managerial strategies

In rejecting the structural determinism of Braverman's industrial model of the labour process, there is a danger of adopting the voluntarist position that a labour process is simply a set of processes negotiated by its participants. For example, Strauss et al. depict the work organisation of a hospital as a 'negotiated order' between various personnel, with the social order in constant flux (Strauss et al., 1963). The concept of 'managerial strategy' may be a way of charting a course through the twin perils of determinism and voluntarism. An emphasis on managerial strategy opens up an approach which neither removes from consideration the work processes in which labour process participants engage and through which they negotiate their participation, nor reduces the labour process solely to participants' day-to-day activities, abstracted from the specific conditions and power relations within which work processes are located. Criticisms of the concept of managerial strategy have been voiced. Rose and Jones criticise the concept by emphasising the 'piecemeal, uncoordinated and empiricist' nature of managerial action (Rose and Jones, 1985, p. 91). However, as Storey argues, Rose and Jones' requirements for the demonstration of the existence of managerial strategies are so stringent that any degree of inconsistency in a managerial strategy, or difficulty experienced by managers in implementing it, is read as evidence of the lack of a strategy to begin with. If less demanding requirements are set managerial strategy can be rescued as a useful concept.

Managers have to work through other people and they presumably have some strategies for how that is to be done and for what they are attempting to achieve. In the private sector, strategies are directed towards the maximisation of surplus value. In the public service sector, strategies are geared to the production of use values determined through political processes. In the latter case, management strategies are located in political, economic and ideological contexts. Public sector managerial strategies may be similar to those of the private sector, but in the public sector they are shaped by policy responses to those contexts, rather than being a response to markets (Dent, 1991, p. 83; Newman and Clarke, 1994, p. 20). If the organisational structure of the labour process is located in these contexts, then political decisions and choices come to the fore and developments in the social work labour process can only be understood in relation to shifts in local and national contexts. For example,   local developments in 'Welfareville's' social work labour process which were driven by the management strategy of decentralisation (see Chapter Six) were   premised on a national framework for   the bureau-professional form of the social work labour process, a framework itself located in the post-war social democratic welfare state (see Chapter Four). This example of a managerial strategy of decentralisation in Welfareville illustrates a general point about managerial strategies. They are expressed in varying configurations of structures and in the processual nature of working practices within those structures. In the case of Welfareville's specific configuration of the bureau-professional social work labour process, senior managerial strategy was pursued through an organisational structure in which the line of authority associated with the hierarchy of classic bureaucracy was both subject to 'breaks' between relatively autonomous levels and existed alongside other alliances and networks.

Another point concerning managerial strategy, which can be illustrated from Chapter Six, is that current managerial strategy has to contend with tensions and contradictions previous managerial strategy has created (Storey, 1983, 1985). In Chapter Six, we saw that Welfareville's senior managers faced what proved to be insuperable problems in attempting to tilt the balance of their strategy away from decentralisation and towards more centralised control of staffing resources through the use of District Audits. This illustration indicates two important points for future work on managerial strategies as a suitable starting point for analysing developments in the social work labour process. First, the labour process will be affected but not necessarily determined by current managerial strategies (Dent, 1991, p. 66). Secondly, managerial strategies have specific time-scales and articulations (Clarke et al., 1994, p. 4) and therefore should be examined in relation to specific historical and current contingencies (Ramsay et al., 1991, p. 35; Smith et al., 1991, p. 6).

Levels in the labour process

Although the post-Braverman debate was vigorous and prolific, few of those who participated presented a rounded account of the labour processes they were studying (Brown, 1992, p. 222). Typically they focused on narrow aspects of the operation of the 'frontier of control' at the point of production (Littler and Salaman, 1982, p. 266). It has been argued in the previous section that managerial strategy is a concept which might provide a suitable starting point for analysing developments in the social work labour process. Addressing the impact of managerial strategy might best be accomplished through more rounded accounts of developments in the labour process provided by detailed scrutiny of the ramifications of strategy at different 'levels in the labour process'. Attention to the different levels in the social work labour process, for example as a way of documenting the recomposition of internal regimes (Newman and Clarke, 1994, p. 24), allows for the analysis of the dominant trends in managerial strategies across different historical periods, whilst avoiding the temptation to fall back into earlier labour process perspective concerns to produce rigid categorisations or historically determined sequences capable of encompassing all sectors and all labour processes. The data presented in earlier chapters suggest it may be wise to establish empirically the form of specific labour processes, rather than deriving them from general categories of analysis related to overarching periodisations of capitalist development.

In the case of the social work labour process, empirical consideration of the labour process's stratification on a number of levels offers potential benefits. Such an approach allows for the analysis of changes *within* levels and changes in the relationship *between* levels over time. For example, as far as relations between the levels of central and local government are concerned, in the period covered by this study of Welfareville once legislation was in place local authority Social Services Departments decided how it was to be implemented in their locality. In the years that have elapsed since the study was completed, major changes have taken place in central-local relations: 'The more the balance of power shifted towards central government in the 1980s, the more it was able to insert its own values, methods and language into the new management practices and the more difficult it became for local institutions to shape the new methods in their own image and for their own purposes' (Burns et al., 1994, p. 85). In relation to Social Services Departments, legislation premised on the requirement to harmonise private and public sector labour processes through the introduction of quasi-markets and the new managerialism has been accompanied by detailed policy and practice 'guidance', with compliance monitored by the Social Services Inspectorate and the Audit Commission (Kelly, 1991; Jones and Novak, 1993).

This brief example illustrates the strength of the claim for the potential benefits to be gained from an analysis of dominant trends in the labour process, within and between levels. However, there is a need to insert a note of caution alongside a claim for the benefits of analysing a changing social work labour process in relation to its constituent levels. In analysing changing trends the potential for continuity and overlap needs to be held against the existence of change. For example, whereas the radical social work literature depicted the shift from the pre-Seebohm to the post-Seebohm era as a critical juncture, represented as a sharp break, this was only accurate in relation to the overall enlarged organisational structure of the new Social Services Departments (local government level). There was considerable continuity in social work practice, through casework (social worker/service user level), and in management methods through the parochial professionalism of supervision (front-line management level). This indicates that the precise nature of present changes in the social work labour process needs to be established through careful analysis and empirical evidence of levels in the labour process and relations between them, if a new version of the radical social work paradigm's determinism is not to be constructed around the new managerialism.

The social work labour process and the service user

Locating the case study presented earlier within the labour process perspective causes some difficulties. All paradigms have limitations created by their focus on those problems which are considered more significant than others (Kuhn, 1970, p. 109). Consideration of an alternative model of the social work labour process began from a proposition that the state was engaged in the production of use values. In retrospect, it is clear that such an approach minimises the potential conflict of interest between service users and social work, stemming from social work's controlling and surveillance functions. Social work's production of use values, or its 'caring' functions, cannot be neatly lopped off from control and surveillance (Clarke, 1979, p. 132). As we saw in Chapter Three, some of the radical social work literature fell into this trap and thence obscured the nature of social worker/service user relations. Bolger et al. argue that as welfare workers have only their labour power to sell they are members of the working class and that '...relations between welfare workers, manual industrial workers and welfare clients are relations within a class and not between classes' (Bolger et al., 1981, p. 22). Accordingly, they argue that welfare workers can be seen as the direct allies of working people (Bolger et al., 1981, p. 99).

Service user movements in their demands for rights and representation based on citizenship (Williams, 1993, p. 98) have drawn attention to social work's implication in the discrimination and oppression service users experience and

Bolger et al.'s assumed coincidence of interests between social workers and service users would now be greeted with suspicion in many quarters. Jones' emphasis on social work's potential as a form of state control (Jones, 1983, Ch. 5) would be regarded as an equally, or more, appropriate starting point to that of the stress on social work's production of use values. To emphasise the social work labour process as concerned with the production of use values, without analysing the ways in which they are distorted, harks back to a social democratic view of state welfare services as in some sense outwith capitalist society. In so doing, the surveillance and controlling functions of the social work labour process are mystified. The social work labour process confers power on social workers as state agents and to regard social workers as only workers, ignores their power over service users (Mishra, 1984, pp. 93-95; Wilding, 1982). It is their position as state agents within the particular labour process of social work which gives social workers a large measure of control over their day-to-day work.

Although a fairly lengthy account of Derber's work on the distinction between ideological and technical subordination was given (see Chapter Four), this account was used mainly to question   the radical social work literature's analysis of the technical subordination alleged to be taking place in the social work labour process. As a consequence,   the significance of social work's ideological incorporation into the state was downplayed. A similar approach was taken in the discussion of levels in the social work labour process (see Chapter Four) with the existence of legislation simply being noted, rather than analysed for its impact on social workers' role as state agents. As this book was not concerned with the detailed operation of either the central government level or the social worker/service user level in the labour process, it could be argued that such omissions are of little consequence. However, in suggesting that front-line managers managed their links with social workers on the basis of a shared parochial professionalism in supervision sessions (see Chapter Seven), what may be significant within this parochial professionalism is the understandings and tensions between front-line managers and social workers about the framework of statutory duties within which discretion and autonomy are exercised.

Future work on the social work labour process needs to acknowledge the power of social workers as state agents. It needs to begin with a conception of the social work labour process as involved in the production of use values interwoven with controlling/ surveillance functions in such a way as to define those 'private troubles' (be they 'personal problems' or 'deviant behaviour') which became public issues and in which the state, through social workers, intervenes.

The labour process perspective and social divisions

In retrospect, the initial decision to locate the study presented earlier within the labour process perspective had other difficulties. Grounding it in the labour process perspective carried with it an assumption about the primacy of class-based economic relations at the workplace, with individuals as personifications of places in the labour process. Such an approach shares with the radical social work texts the propensity to side-step questions about the categories of people who occupy the places in the labour process and the categories of service users with whom they work. Women (lesbian or heterosexual), Black people, gay men, older people and people with disabilities - whether as social workers or as service users - were almost completely absent from the white, male-dominated radical social work paradigm of the traditional Left (Hearn, 1982a, p. 23; Frost and Stein, 1989, p.34; Langan and Lee, 1989, p. 5; Day, 1992, p. 12; Langan, 1992, p. 3). How does the labour process interlock with social divisions generated by structures of oppression other than class?

In considering the role of strategic choice in the labour process, Whittington argues that the structures of class, gender and ethnicity restrict strategic choice to a narrow circle (Whittington, 1988, pp. 532-533). More widely, Hugman points out that 'The work which people undertake, whether or not they are professionally qualified, the hierarchical positions they occupy and so on are all linked, and all these factors are related to whether the person is Black or white, female or male' (Hugman, 1991, p. 204). In future work, first, the operation of discrimination in labour markets needs to be brought into the labour process perspective (Thompson and McHugh, 1990, p. 293). Williams, for example, has analysed the structuring of welfare state labour markets along class, 'race' and gender lines (Williams, 1991). Secondly, the discriminatory nature of labour markets needs to be supplemented by analysing the impact of social divisions within the operation of the labour process. Hearn and Parkin's stress on the significance of broader power relationships in relation to sexuality, for example, points to women as a threat to male identity in the workplace. Instrumental working relationships reinforce patriarchy and sexism through desexualising the nature of work organisations (Hearn and Parkin, 1987, p.19). This example raises broader questions about the way in which abled/disabled, ethnic, gendered, generational and sexual identities shape and constrain the experience of the social work labour process.

Work undertaken on the significance of social divisions in social work has mushroomed in the period since this study was completed. The utilisation of a labour process perspective might carry such work forward. One of the striking features of much of the work undertaken on social divisions is its emphasis on developing a series of radical agendas, generated by the experience of a range of social divisions. This emphasis has been accompanied by a lack of attention to contextualising the changes the agendas demand in the labour process of social work. But, unless work on social divisions is located within the structure and processes within which change is to be achieved, there will be no sustained analysis of the nooks and crannies of contradictions and tensions in the labour process, within which there might be room for manoeuvre in realising some of the items on radical agendas. Connecting social divisions to the significance of social work as *work*, would help to avoid slipping into empty rhetoric or the assertion of the necessity for principles, values and attitudes which are detached from an analysis of how they might be realised within specific labour processes. Consideration of employment issues and practice issues needs to be brought together (Kirwan, 1994, p. 139). Social divisions which shape participation in, and are embedded in the operation of, the labour process have been obscured in the labour process perspective (Smith et al., 1991, pp. 411-412), whereas in social work's analysis of social divisions and anti-discriminatory practice, the labour process itself has often been obscured.

The four areas discussed, do not exhaust the possible contribution of labour process analysis to social work or of social work to the labour process perspective. They do, however, emphasise that the labour process perspective still has a role to play as a critical paradigm for social work, to be employed in the analysis of the structure and process of its labour process in specific historical and political contexts.

Appendix: The sample of front-line managers

Introduction

This appendix provides information on the sample of front-line managers interviewed in the case study of Welfareville and gives an outline of their work histories. It is axiomatic that individual District Manager's work histories in Welfareville did not exist in an organisational vacuum but are related to the constraints and opportunities of the structure of the labour process in which they are located (Brown, 1982, pp. 123-7), as set out in Chapter Six.

Table 1
Employment as a front-line manager in Welfareville as a percentage of post-qualification experience

Sam	80%
Irene	77%
Grant	75%
Curtis	71%
Campbell	68%
Jonah	52%
Michael	45%
Brian	45%
Carlton	44%
Ivan	44%
Tim	38%
Charles	36%
Jamie	18%
Tina	18%

Table 1 sets out the amount of time the sample had spent as front-line managers in Welfareville Social Services Department, as a percentage of their post-qualifying experience, and indicates that twelve of the sample had been front-line managers in Welfareville for between one third and four-fifths of the time following qualification.

Table 2
Total period of employment in Welfareville as a percentage of
post-qualification experience

Tina	100%
Irene	100%
Ivan	100%
Grant	100%
Sam	100%
Tim	80%
Carlton	78%
Michael	76%
Jonah	73%
Jamie	68%
Campbell	68%
Curtis	48%
Charles	36%
Brian	36%

Table 2 sets out the amount of time the District Managers had spent employed in Welfareville Social Services Department and its predecessor departments, prior to and including their employment as front-line managers, as a percentage of their post-qualifying experience.

Gender

Women

Two of the sample of District Managers were women. The position of women has received relatively little attention compared to that of men in the labour process perspective.

When we approach the organisational structure of the social work labour process, it is clear that it has been a male-dominated, vertically segregated structure, with women disproportionately concentrated in the ranks of basic grade

131

social worker and men over-represented in the echelons of management, including front-line management.   Brown identifies four factors which he suggests traditionally affected women's orientations to work: firstly, primary socialisation to marriage as a career in itself; secondly, restricted opportunities when entering employment; thirdly, women's domestic responsibilities; fourthly, being located in jobs with few opportunities for intrinsic job satisfaction (Brown, 1982).

When we consider the work histories of the two District Managers who were women, the force of these factors becomes clear.   Both of the women entered employment when they left school at 15.   Irene had a break from employment outside the home in an office when her children were born.   When she re-entered employment she entered social work via a 'low-status' route: as a welfare officer in Welfareville's pre-Seebohm Welfare Department.   In the Social Services Department she moved form Home Help Organiser to Welfare Assistant to Social Worker to District Manager.   When Tina married her employment at a bank, which she had joined on leaving school, was abruptly terminated, in accordance with the bank's rules concerning the dismissal of women who married.   She then had several different jobs in which she alternated between working as a technician and as a bookkeeper before securing a place on a social work training course and then becoming a social worker and a District Manager. Irene gave this account of her motivation for seeking a post as District Manager:

> I applied for the job because I was very critical of senior management at the time.   I think now that a lot of my criticisms were justified because a lot of people were promoted 1971-73, not because of their competence to do senior posts but because there weren't many qualified staff about.   There was rapid promotion and not always the best people got promotion.   We had a number of people appointed to senior posts who weren't competent enough.   That influenced me.

In terms of future aspirations, both Irene and Tina were 'non-careerists' (Hearn, 1977). Irene thought she was in a difficult position.   She had reservations about continuing as a front-line manager but felt she was committed to her identity as a District Manager in the eyes of others, because by applying for promotion she had made a statement about where she saw her future.   To divest herself of her position would also be accompanied by a loss of self-esteem.   She felt constrained therefore to accept her continuation in the post, in the spirit of accepting a life-sentence:

> I'm not sure whether I made the right decision to come into this job...I would like to return to practice.   When anybody outside asks me what I do, I say I'm a social worker.   I don't think it's made easy for people to stand down.

Tina was equally ambivalent:

It's difficult being a District Manager. The whole spectrum of social work lands on the D.M.'s desk. Everybody's problems. I don't want the job. You've got to be able to give a lot more time than I'm prepared to give to the job. You've got to be more committed than I am and I don't want my job to rule my life. I think it does when you're a D.M. and it certainly has for me for the last twelve months. You don't finish when you go home. You take papers home with you because you don't have the chance to read them during the day. You write reports at home.

It was impossible to estimate from the interview transcripts   the relative influence of long-standing gender differences in Tina's and Irene's experience of work as against the stress their male managers may have created for them.   Neither complained of their treatment by male managers, but it might have been that their general comments about the demands of their jobs concealed a lack of support from managers in recognising the importance of their domestic worlds in relation to their work: a lack of support of which they themselves might have been unaware, but which they took for granted as part of the expectations of the (male) organisational structure. What is clear is the extent to which factors outside work had influenced, and continued to influence, their work history. This was very different from the men's accounts of their experiences.

Men

For the men I interviewed, home and work appeared to be regarded as distinct worlds. There did not seem to be the same emphasis, as for the two women, on balancing the demands of work and domestic responsibilities, even though all but two were married. Only Brian even mentioned home/children, when he stated that he would think twice about a career move which would disturb his children's secondary education. For the men, their work history was presented as either being, or having been, a challenge; a challenge not just to obtain a post with greater status but an opportunity to develop their creative powers. Their references to the 'challenge', 'creativity' and 'buzz' of work implied that their work histories provided their lives with a purpose and a structure and gave them an enhanced view of themselves.

There were three work history patterns amongst the men: first, change of direction. Jamie, Sam, Curtis, Tim and Michael had entered social work after substantial periods of employment elsewhere: Jamie as an artist, Sam as an electrical engineer, Curtis as a nurse, Tim as a schoolteacher and Michael after working in a factory. Second, Grant, Ivan, Brian and Jonah had gone to University straight from school (three of them to Oxbridge) and then chosen further courses of education which made them acceptable as entrants to social work. Third, Campbell, Carlton, and Charles after completing undergraduate degrees had a delayed entry into social work. Campbell was unemployed and

Charles and Carlton undertook jobs they regarded as temporary before all three chose further courses of education which enabled them to enter social work.

Cosmopolitans and locals

Gouldner noted two approaches to the achievement of successful work history strategies, those of 'cosmopolitans' and 'locals' (Gouldner, 1954) or in Brown's terms, 'occupational' and 'organisational' strategies, Brown, 1982).   The two women were 'locals' and the men split 50/50 into District Managers who had been 'cosmopolitans' and 'locals' to date. The six male 'cosmopolitans' talked about their work histories leading up to their appointment as District Managers as steps in a career. All six described the 'pull' factor of the reputation of Welfareville's Social Services Department:

> [Brian] 'The attraction was the Department's reputation'.

> [Curtis] 'There was a lot of good publicity about the Department and all the things it was doing.'

For four of the cosmopolitans, the general appeal of the Department's reputation was heightened by its policy of decentralising services:

> [Campbell] 'I liked the decentralised model'.

> [Charles] 'I liked the size of the decentralised patch.'

The six male and two female 'locals', all of whom who were internally promoted, made reference to their promotion as the logical outcome of a sequential process of growing awareness of their own ability and a desire to change the style of management in the Department. They presented this process as a gradual pressure in the direction of becoming a District Manager. This view of promotion contrasts strongly with that of the cosmopolitans, who were much more candid in discussing their desire for promotion. It may be that the locals were employing their gradualist accounts to rationalise the uneasiness and ambiguous status which often accompanies internal promotion, or it may be that the cosmopolitans were more career-conscious. These extracts reflect the process described by locals:

> [Carlton] 'I'd been a practitioner for ten years and it was only in the last three years as a practitioner that I became interested in the problems of management. Before I was very anti-management. I was very much the individual, analytically-oriented social worker. I got to the point where I wanted to do something about management, instead of just reacting against it. I also thought

that I had something to offer as a supervisor. I wanted to move management
and supervision down to a more practice, client-centred basis'.

[Jamie] 'I saw it in terms of being a voice for a group of people who receive
information first hand, feeding through information pertaining to services and
resources. I thought that information wasn't being passed to the powers that
be'.

[Ivan] 'I saw this job as offering the opportunity to be more involved in policy
development than I could be as a practitioner, so I think that the initial
attraction was to have more say over the development of social services. It
would mean more scope than I would have as a practitioner.'

Thus, whilst cosmopolitan entrants to the post of District Manager presented their
move as the logical next step in their careers, the motivations of local entrants to
the post were presented by them as more hesitant and complex.
  Given the finding in Satyamurti's study that 'many social workers said that the
anticipation of being promoted was all that kept them going, since they did not feel
they could tolerate an indefinite period in the field' (Satyamurti, 1980, p. 37), it is
surprising to find that only Carlton said he was disillusioned with practice, and
then only mildly so: 'As a generic practitioner, I could only see more of the same
coming up and I was becoming a bit routinised. The loneliness of the long-distant
social worker!'
  Two of the locals were in a different position to the other four. Grant and Sam
were promoted in the Seebohm re-organisation, Sam from the Children's
Department, Grant from the Mental health Department:

[Sam] 'When Social Services was formed I was appointed a Senior Social
Worker. I've been in the same post right the way through. Fifteen seniors had
to be appointed. They were chosen on a numerical basis from each of the old
departments'.

[Grant] 'I was brought into this team as the Senior Social Worker on
reorganisation, having been a basic grade social worker for a number of years.
It was something I saw as a natural progression and certainly there was
encouragement for me to apply as well. It was very much part of the general
movement that was going on at the time. Some of the most highly qualified
social workers around were in the Mental Welfare Department and there was
an expectation that mental health social workers would do quite well in the new
set-up.'

Careerists

In terms of future aspirations there were six 'careerists' who saw their future in terms of further promotion. All of them were men in their mid-30s. They were at pains to point out that this was not to be promotion at any price:

> [Carlton] 'I've done better than I thought I would as a district manager, and I would like to become a more senior manager. I am trying to move that way but I wouldn't move into a situation where you had complex cases and inexperienced workers or no resources and an overwhelming workload, because that would be unmanageable by definition. There is no point taking on a job and pretending to do a job which can't be done.'

The motivation for further promotion was presented in terms of enlarged scope for policy development including space for personal creativity:

> [Ivan] 'One of the frustrations of this job is that I don't have an hour or two to work on something uninterrupted. Maybe it's a fantasy but I would quite' like to do that, to work on producing reports. I quite enjoy spending time looking at policy issues, producing documents and all that sort of thing. When I look to the future, if I could actually get some kind of job that would be less pressurised and potentially more satisfying. One possibility is an Area Director's job ...I don't want to take on a job which I don't feel I can take within my stride and I want to feel that I have got something clearly to offer'.

> [Jonah] 'I see myself going higher. One of the things I get a kick out of from this job is the potential for being quite creative. I really enjoy the creativity. I think it's a work of art in a sense. You work with a diverse group of people and you can spot things that people need help on. Helping to make things happen. Moving things along. I would like to do that on a bigger scale, so I do see myself going further. I would enjoy doing that on a bigger scale with larger units.'

If we examine these statements about involvement in policy development and increased scope for creativity, it is apparent that what these District Managers were seeking was more influence over other levels in the labour process. In Social Services Departments power (or 'personal creativity') is often exercised over issues, by reference to how outcomes should be determined in the light of the Department's policies. These District Managers see themselves as being able to exercise more influence over the labour process by moving beyond the front-line level.   The problem for these aspiring managers is that they experience considerable autonomy in interpreting and adapting policy as front-line managers over the local level of the labour process, an autonomy they would have to relinquish in order to advance:

> [Michael] 'It's difficult for me to look up into the hierarchy and see a job which offers more opportunities than I have at the moment because of the degree of autonomy I have. I have the power to get involved in things and to play a significant role in making things happen. It's difficult to see that in the immediate step above me.'

At the time of the research, the prospects for the (male) careerists were beginning to look much less a smooth path of progression than they might have anticipated in the boom years of Social Services Departments for a number of reasons. First, the expansion of Social Services Departments had either levelled off, as was the case in Welfareville, or had declined in many others. In other words, the opportunity structure had contracted. Secondly, it could no longer be assumed that women who possessed the same qualifications as men, would not be promoted. Thirdly, the level of 'human capital' amongst women was increasing. The (male) careerists were faced, therefore, with the problem of adjusting their aspirations to their actual opportunities. At the time of the research, the careerists did not feel behind on the 'career clock'. However, as time went on there would presumably be considerable bunching of people of roughly the same age at front-line management level. This development had the potential to generate considerable tension in the organisation, as the District Managers increasingly considered their abilities to be under-utilised and found what they regarded as their legitimate aspirations frustrated. The trend described by Jonah may become more pronounced:

> I think in the past there have been career issues in terms of people like myself who have been in post. People have seen senior management as the group to which they look and the group which they would want to join. You don't poke in the eye groups you want to join, not if you want to join them. In some sense that has diminished because of the lack of job opportunities. The opportunities for District Managers are so few now that there is less of that sort of thinking about.

Non-careerists

Kets de Vries makes a statement which illuminates the position of the (male) non-careerists:

> As the manager gets more settled in his (sic) career, a timetable of expectations evolves, tracking progress in working life, on this 'career clock' we find critical

points such as possible dates of advancement...By positioning himself (sic) on the career clock the manager is constantly assessing his (sic) progress over the career life cycle and evaluating whether he (sic) is ahead or behind schedule...Most managers will come to some form of halt in their career (Kets de Vries, 1980, p. 145).

Grant and Sam regarded their careers as having come to a halt. They had occupied the same, albeit changing, post for twelve years at the time of the research. They had seen other District Managers come and go. One of their contemporaries was the Deputy Director of the Department and, shortly after the research was completed, he became the Director. In comparing their occupational fate to that of others, both thought that they had little hope of promotion, even though they had made attempts in the past. They seemed to regard acceptance of their position as a release from one source of pressure and considered there were benefits in the situation:

[Sam] 'Being a DM is one of the best jobs in the Department. You've got a lot of autonomy but if you keep your nose clean you don't get bothered. It's a very nice job and I like it. I've been in it so long that I can almost free-wheel';

[Grant] 'Over the years when there have been Area Manager vacancies, I've seen that as the logical next step. But maybe I'm not regarded as a manager. I'm certainly not regarded as a potential senior manager in the Department. I imagine that my feelings about the practice element of the job show through pretty clearly, and that is something which probably goes against me when I am applying for senior posts. I'm ambivalent about it any way because I'm not sure that the Area Manager's job is something that I would really want. I suppose that given the set-up in the Department, the DM's job is the one best suited to me and the one that I can do best. I do sometimes think about the possibility of returning to practice but there's obviously the question of salary and my commitments outside the job. It probably means I'll be staying where I am.'

Both Sam and Grant referred to important interests outside work. Sam to his activities as his wife's consort, as she was the Mayor of a local town, and Grant to his involvement in voluntary organisations.

Curtis had occupied his post as a District Manager for nine years and a similar one for four years before that in another local authority. Although he had taken a course which was aimed at preparing people to be Area Managers, he said that 'around two years ago I made a decision that this was as far as I want to go in social services. I have other interests in life.'

Three others claimed to be non-careerists but within six months of their research interviews had applied for, and moved into, more senior posts.

Bibliography

Abbott, P. and Wallace, C. (1990), *An Introduction to Sociology: Feminist Perspectives*, Routledge: London.

Abercrombie, N. and Urry, J. (1983), *Capital, Labour and the Middle Classes*, Allen and Unwin: London.

Algie, J. (1975), *Social Values, Objectives and Action*, Kogan Page: London.

Anthias, F. (1980), 'Women and the Reserve Army of Labour', *Capital and Class*, 10, pp. 127-142.

Audit Commission (1988), *The Competitive Council*, HMSO: London.

Bailey, R. and Brake, M. (eds) (1975), *Radical Social Work*, Edward Arnold: London.

Bailey, R. and Brake, M. (1980), 'Contributions to a Radical Practice in Social Work', in Brake, M. and Bailey, R. (eds) *Radical Social Work and Practice*, Edward Arnold: London.

Bain, G.S., Coates, D. and Ellis, V. (1973), *Social Stratification and Trade Unionism*, Heinemann: London.

Bains Report (1972), *The New Local Authorities. Report of the Study Group on Local Authority Management Structure*, HMSO: London.

Bamford, T. (1982), *Managing Social Work*, Tavistock: London.

Bamford, T. (1989), 'Discretion and Managerialism' in Sharlow, S. (Ed) *The Values of Change in Social Work*, Tavistock/Routledge: London.

Barclay, P. (Chair) (1982), *Social Workers: Their Roles and Tasks*, National Institute for Social Work/Bedford Square Press: London.

Baxandall, R., Ewen, E. and Gordan, L. (1976), 'The Working Class Has Two Sexes', *Monthly Review*, 28, 3, pp. 24-35.

Beechey, V. (1982), 'The Sexual Division of Labour and the Labour Process', in Wood, S. (Ed) *The Degradation of Work: Skill, Deskilling and the Labour Process*, Hutchison: London.

Beechey, V. (1987), *Unequal Work*. London, Verso.

Bell, C. and Newby, H. (eds) (1980), *Doing Sociological Research*, Allen and Unwin: London.

Bell, C. and Roberts, H. (eds) (1984), *Social Researching. Politics, Problems, Practice*, R.K.P.: London.

Benington, J. (1976), *Local Government Becomes Big Business*, Home Office, Community Development Project: London.

Bennett, B. (1980), 'The Sub-office: A Team Approach to Local Authority Fieldwork Practice', in Brake, M. and Bailey, R. (eds) *Radical Social Work and Practice*, Edward Arnold: London.

Berg, M. (ed) (1979), *Technology and Toil in Nineteenth Century Britain*, CSE Books: London.

Beynon, H. (1973), *Working for Ford*, Penguin: Harmondsworth.

Bittner, E. (1986), 'The Police on Skid Row: A Study of Peace-keeping' in Salaman, G. and Thompson, K. (eds) *People and Organisations*, Longman: London.

Black, J., Bowl, R., Burns, D., Critcher, C., Grant, G. and Stockford, D. (1983), *Social Work in Context*, Tavistock: London.

Blackburn, R.M., Prandy, K. and Stewart, A.L. (1974), 'Concepts and Measures: The Example of Unionateness', *Sociology*, 8, 2, pp. 427-446.

Blau, P. (1963), *The Dynamics of Bureaucracy*, University of Chicago: Chicago.

Blau, P. and Scott, W. (1963), *Formal Organisations: A Comparative Approach*, R.K.P.: London.

Blyton, P. and Ursell, G. (1982), 'Vertical Recruitment in White Collar Trade Unions: Some Causes and Consequences', *British Journal of Industrial Relations*, July 1982.

Bolger, S., Corrigan, P., Docking, J., and Frost, N. (1981), *Towards Socialist Welfare Work. Working in the State*, Macmillan: London.

Bradley, H. (1986), 'Technological Change, Management Strategies, and the Development of Gender-Based Job Segregation in the Labour Process', in Knights, D. and Willmott, H. (eds) *Gender and the Labour Process*, Gower: Aldershot.

Brake, M. and Bailey, R. (eds) (1980), *Radical Social Work and Practice*, Edward Arnold: London.

Braverman, H. (1974), *Labor and Monopoly Capital: The Degradation of Work in the Twentieth Century*, Monthly Review Press: New York.

Bresnen, M. (1988), 'Insights on Site' in Bryman, A. (ed) *Doing Research in Organisations*, Routledge: London.

Brooke, R. (1989), 'The Enabling Authority: Practical Consequences', *Local Government Studies*, 15, 5, pp. 55-63.

Brown, R. (1982), 'Work Histories, Career Strategies and the Class Structure', in Giddens, A. and Mackenzie, G. (eds) *Social Class and the Division of Labour*, Cambridge University Press: Cambridge.

Brown, R. (1992), *Understanding Industrial Organisations. Theoretical Perspectives in Industrial Sociology*, Routledge: London.

Bruegel, I. (1979), 'Women as a Reserve Army of Labour: A Note on Recent British Experience', *Feminist Review*, 1, 3, pp. 12-23.

Bryman, A. (1989), *Research Methods and Organisation Studies*, Unwin Hyman: London.

Bryman, A. and Burgess, R.G. (eds) (1994), *Analysing Qualitative Data*, Routledge: London.

Buchanan, D.A. (1986), 'Management Objectives in Technical Change', in Knights, D. and Willmott, H. (eds), *Managing the Labour Process*, Gower: Aldershot.

Buckle, J. (1981), *Intake Teams*, Tavistock: London.

Burawoy, M. (1978), 'Towards a Marxist Theory of the Labour Process: Braverman and Beyond', *Politics and Society*, 8, 3, pp. 48-53.

Burawoy, M. (1979), *Manufacturing Consent: Changes in the Labor Process under Monopoly Capitalism*, University of Chicago Press: Chicago.

Burawoy, M. (1985), *The Politics of Production*, Verso: London.

Burns, D., Hambleton, R. and Hoggett, P. (1994), *The Politics of Decentralisation*, Macmillan: Basingstoke.

Carchedi, G. (1977), *On the Economic Identification of Social Classes*, R.K.P.: London.

Carr-Saunders, A.M. and Wilson, P.A. (1962), *The Professions*, Oxford University Press: London.

Carter, R. (1979), 'Class Militancy and Union Character', *Sociological Review*, 27, pp. 137-151.

Case Con (1975), 'Case Con Manifesto', reprinted in Bailey, R. and Brake, M. (eds) (1980), *Radical Social Work*, Edward Arnold: London.

Cavendish, R. (1982), *Women on the Line*, Routledge and Kegan Paul: London.

Cawson, A. (1982), *Corporatism and Welfare*, Heinemann: London.

Challis, L. (1990), *Organising Public Social Services,*Longman: Harlow.

Child, J. (1985), 'Managerial Strategies, New Technology and the Labour Process', in Knights, D., Willmott, H. and Collinson, D. (eds) *Job Redesign. Critical Perspectives on the Labour Process*, Gower: Aldershot.

Child, J. and Partridge, B. (1982), *Lost Managers: Supervisors in Industry*, Cambridge University Press: Cambridge.

Clark, C.L. and Asquith, S. (1975), *Social Work and Social Philosophy*, R.K.P.: London.

Clarke, J. (1979), 'Critical Sociology and Radical Social Work: Problems of Theory and Practice' in Parry, N., Rustin, M. and Satyamurti, C. (eds) *Social Work Welfare and the State*, Edward Arnold: London.

Clarke, J. (ed) (1993), *A Crisis in Care? Challenges to Social Work*, Sage: London.

Clarke, J., Cochrane, A. and McLaughlin, E. (eds) (1994a), *Managing Social Policy*, Sage: London.

Clarke, J., Cochrane, A. and McLaughlin, E. (1994b), 'Introduction: Why Management Matters', in Clarke, J., Cochrane, A. and McLaughlin, E. (eds) *Managing Social Policy*, Sage: London.

Clarke, J., Cochrane, A. and McLaughlin, E. (1994c), 'Mission Accomplished or Unfinished Business? The Impact of Managerialisation', in Clarke, J., Cochrane, A. and McLaughlin, E. (eds) *Managing Social Policy*, Sage: London.

Clarke, J. and Langan, M. (1993a), 'The British Welfare State: Foundation and Modernisation', in Cochrane, A. and Clarke, J. (eds) *Comparing Welfare States. Britain in International Context*, Sage: London.

Clarke, J. and Langan, M. (1993b), 'Restructuring Welfare: The British Welfare Regime in the 1980s', in Cochrane, A. and Clarke, J. (eds) *Comparing Welfare States. Britain in International Context*, Sage: London.

Clarke, J. and Newman, J. (1993), 'Managing to Survive; Dilemmas of Changing Organisational Forms in the Public Sector', in Deakin, N. and Page, R., *The Costs of Welfare*, Avebury: Aldershot.

Clegg, S. and Dunkerley, D. (1980), *Organisation, Class and Control*, Routledge and Kegan Paul: London.

Cochrane, A. (1994), 'Managing Change in Local Government', in Clarke, J., Cochrane, A. and McLaughlin, E. (eds), *Managing Social Policy*, Sage: London.

Cochrane, A. and Clarke, J. (eds) (1993), *Comparing Welfare States. Britain in International Context*, Sage: London.

Cockburn, C. (1977), *The Local State. The Management of Cities and People*, Pluto: London.

Cockburn, C. (1983), *Brothers: Male Dominance and Technological Change*, Pluto: London.

Cohen, S. (1975), 'It's All Right For You To Talk', in Bailey, R. and Brake, M. (eds) *Radical Social Work*, Edward Arnold: London.

Cohen, S. (1987), 'A Labour Process to Nowhere?', *New Left Review*, 107, pp. 34-50.

Coombs, R. (1978), 'Labour and Monopoly Capital', *New Left Review*, 107, pp.79-96.

Cooper, J. (1983), *The Creation of the British Social Services, 1962-1974*, Heinemann: London.

Cooper, J. (1991), 'The Future of Social work: A Pragmatic View', in Loney, M., Bocock, R., Clarke, J., Cochrane, A., Graham, P. and Wilson, M., *The State or the Market. Politics and Welfare in Contemporary Britain*, Sage: London.

Corrigan, P. and Leonard, P. (1978), *Social Work Practice Under Capitalism: A Marxist Approach*, Macmillan: London.

Cousins, C. (1987), *Controlling Social Welfare: a Sociology of State Welfare Work and Organisation*, Wheatsheaf: Brighton.

Coyle, A. (1982), *Redundant Women*, The Women's Press: London.

Cressey, P. and MacInnes, J. (1980), 'Voting for Ford: Industrial Democracy and the Control of Labour', *Capital and Class*, 11, pp. 5-37.

Crewe, I. (1982), 'The Labour Party and the Electorate', in Kavanagh D. (ed) *The Politics of the Labour Party*, Allen and Unwin: London.

Crompton, R. and Jones, G. (1984), *White Collar Proletariat*, Macmillan: London.

Crompton, R. and Reid, S. (1982), 'The De-skilling of Clerical Work', in Wood, S. (ed) *The Degradation of Work: Skill, De-skilling and the Labour Process*, Hutchison: London.

Crouch, C. (1982), *Trade Unions: The Logic of Collective Action*, Fontana: London.

Davey, I. (1977), 'Radical Social Work - What Does it Mean in Practice?' , *Social Work Today*, 8, p. 23.

Day, L. (1992), 'Women and Oppression: Race, Class and Gender', in Langan, M. and Day, L. *Women, Oppression and Social Work*, Routledge: London.

Dent, M. (1991), 'Autonomy and the Medical Profession: Medical Audit and Management Control', in Smith, C. Knights, D. and Willmott, H. (1991) *White-Collar Work. The Non-Manual Labour Process*, Macmillan: Basingstoke.

Derber, C. (1982), 'Managing Professionals: Ideological Proletarianisation and Mental Labor', in Derber, C. (ed) *Professionals as Workers: Mental Labor in Advanced Capitalism*, G.K. Hall: Boston.

Derber, C. (1983), 'Managing Professionals: Ideological Proletarianisation and Post- industrial Labor', *Theory and Society*, 12, 3, pp. 309-341.

Dex, S. (1985), *The Sexual Division of Work*, Harvester: Brighton.

Dex, S. (1987), *Women's Occupational Mobility*, Macmillan: Basingstoke.

D.H.S.S. (1971), *Local Authority Social Services Ten Year Plans 1973-1983*, Circular 35/72.

D.H.S.S. (1976), *Priorities in the Health and Personal Social Services*, H.M.S.O.: London.

Doyal, L. and Harris, R. (1986), *Empiricism, Explanation and Rationality. An Introduction to the Philosophy of the Social Sciences*, Routledge Kegan Paul: London.

Dunkerley, D. (1988), 'Historical Methods and Organisational Analysis: The Case of a Naval Dockyard', in Bryman, A. (ed) *Doing Research in Organisations*, Routledge: London.

Edwards, R. (1979), *Contested Terrain; The Transformation of the Workplace in the Twentieth Century*, Heinemann: London.

Elcock, H. (1993), 'Local Government', in Farnham, D. and Horton, S. (eds) *Managing the New Public Services*, Macmillan: Basingstoke.

Elger, T. (1982), 'Braverman, Capital Accumulation and De-skilling', in Wood, S. (ed) *The Degradation of Work: Skill, De-skilling and the Labour Process*, Hutchison: London.

Etzioni, A. (ed) (1969), *The Semi-professions and their Organisation*, Free Press: New York.

Flynn, N. (1993), *Public Sector Management*, Harvester Wheatsheaf: Hemel Hempstead.

Flynn, N. (1994), 'Control, Commitment and Contracts', in Clarke, J., Cochrane, A. and McLaughlin, E. (eds) *Managing Social Policy*, Sage: London.

Friedman, A. (1977a), *Industry and Labour: Class Struggle at Work and Monopoly Capital*, Macmillan: London.

Friedman, A. (1977b), 'Responsible Autonomy versus Direct Control over the Labour Process', *Capital and Class*,1, pp. 27-42.

Frost, N. and Stein, M. (1989), 'What's Happening in Social Services Departments?', in Langan, M. and Lee, P. (eds) *Radical Social Work Today*, Unwin Hyman: London.

Garrett, M. (1980), 'The Problem with Authority', in Brake, M. and Bailey, R. (eds), *Radical Social Work and Practice*, Edward Arnold: London.

Giddens, A. (1979), *Central Problems in Sociological Theory. Action, Structure and Contradiction in Social Analysis*, Macmillan: Basingstoke.

Giddens, A. (1982), 'Power, the Dialectic of Control and Class Structuration', in Giddens, A. and Mackenzie, G. (eds) *Social Class and the Division of Labour*, Cambridge University Press: Cambridge.

Glastonbury, B. (1982), 'The Inalienable Context', in Glastonbury, B., Cooper, D. and Hawkins, P. *Social Work in Conflict - The Practitioner and the Bureaucrat*, B.A.S.W.: Birminghm.

Glastonbury, B., Cooper, D. and Hawkins, P. (1982), *Social Work in Conflict - The Practitioner and the Bureaucrat*, B.A.S.W.: Birmingham.

Goldberg, E.M. and Warburton, R.W. (1979), *Means and Ends in Social Work*, Allen and Unwin: London.

Goldthorpe, J. (1982), 'On the Service Class, its Formation and Future', in Giddens, A. and Mackenzie, G. (eds) *Social Class and the Division of Labour*, Cambridge University Press: Cambridge.

Goldthorpe, J.H., Lockwood, D., Bechofer, F. and Platt, J. (1968), *The Affluent Worker: Industrial Attitudes and Behaviour*, Cambridge University Press: Cambridge.

Gorz, A. (ed) (1976), *The Division of Labour: the Labour Process and Class Struggle in Modern Capitalism*, Harvester: Brighton.

Gospel, H. and Littler, C.R. (1983), *Managerial Strategies and Industrial Relations*, Heinemann: London.

Gough, I. (1979), *The Political Economy of the Welfare State*, Macmillan, London.

Gould, A. (1980), 'The Salaried Middle Class in the Welfare State', *Policy and Politics*, 9, pp. 35-49.

Gouldner, A. (1954), *Patterns of Industrial Bureaucracy*, Free Press: New York.

Gouldner, A. (1971), *The Coming Crisis of Western Sociology*, Heinemann: London.

Greenwood, E. (1957), 'Attributes of a Profession', *Social Work*, 2, 3, pp. 44-55.

Greenwood, R. (1983), 'Changing Patterns of Budgeting in English Local Government', *Public Administration*, 61, pp. 149-168.

Greenwood, R. and Stewart, J.D. (1974), *Corporate Planning in English Local Government*, University of Birmingham, INLOGOV: Birmingham.

Greenwood, R., Walsh, K., Hinings, C. and Ranson, S. (1980), *Patterns of Management in Local Government*, Martin Robertson: Oxford.

Gutek, B., Nakamura, C.U. and Nieva, B.G. (1981), 'The Interdependence of Work and Family Roles', *Journal of Occupational Behaviour*, 2, 1, pp.15-24.

Habermas, J. (1976), *Legitimation Crisis*, Heinemann: London.

Hakim, C. (1979), *Occupational Segregation*, Research Paper No. 9., Department of Employment, H.M.S.O.: London.

Hales, M. (1980), *Living Thinkwork: Where Do Labour Processes Come From?*, CSE Books: London.

Hall, A. (1975), 'Policy-making: More Judgement than Luck', *Community Care*, 6th August.

Hall, P. (1976), *Reforming the Welfare*, Heinemann: London.

Hallett, C. (1982), *The Personal Social Services in Local Government*, Allen and Unwin: London.

Hallett, C. and Stevenson, O. (1980), *Child Abuse*, Allen and Unwin: London.

Hammond, P. (ed) (1964), *Sociologists at Work*, Basic Books: New York.

Handler, J. (1968), *The Coercive Social Worker*, Oxford University Press: Oxford.

Hartmann, H. (1979), 'The Unhappy Marriage of Marxism and Feminism: Towards a More Progressive Union', *Capital and Class*, 8, pp. 1-33.

Hearn, J. (1977), 'Toward a Concept of Non-career', *Sociological Review*, 25, 2, pp. 16-29.

Hearn, J. (1982a), 'Radical Social Work - Contradictions, Limitations and Political Possibilities', *Critical Social Policy*, 2, 1, pp. 19-38.

Hearn, J. (1982b), 'Notes on Patriarchy, Professionalisation and the Semi-professions', *Sociology*, 16, pp. 475-490.

Hearn, J. and Jones, B. (1981), 'Radical Social Work and the Problem of Management', *Community Care*, 367, pp. 13-14.

Hearn, J. and Parkin, W. (1987), *Sex at Work: The Power and Paradox of Organisation Sexuality*, Wheatsheaf: Brighton.

Higgins, J. (1980), 'Social Control Theories of Social Policy', *Journal of Social Policy*, 9, 1, pp. 1-23.

Home Office (1965), *The Child, the Family and the Young Offender*, Cmnd. 2742, H.M.S.O.: London.

Hoggett, P. (1991), 'A New Management in the Public Sector?', *Policy and Politics*, 19, 4, pp. 243-256.

Hoggett, P. and Hambleton, R. (1987), *Decentralisation and Democracy*, University of Bristol, School of Advanced Urban Studies: Bristol.

Hopper, T., Cooper, D., Lowe, T., Capps, T. and Mouritsen, J. (1986), 'Management Control and Worker Resistance in the National Coal Board: Financial Controls in the Labour Process', in Knights, D. and Willmott, H. (eds) *Managing the Labour Process*, Gower: Aldershot.

Howe, D. (1986a), *Social Workers and their Practice in Welfare Bureaucracies*, Gower: Aldershot.

Howe, D. (1986b), 'The Segregation of Women and their Work in the Personal Social Services', *Critical Social Policy*, 15, pp. 21-35.

Hugman, R. (1991), *Power in Caring Professions*, Macmillan: Basingstoke.

Hyman, R. (1971), *Marxism and the Sociology of Trade Unionism*, Pluto: London.

Ingleby (Chair) (1960), *Report of the Committee on Children and Young Persons*, Cmnd. 1191, H.M.S.O.: London.

Jamous, H. and Peloille, B. (1970), 'Changes in the French University-hospital system', in Jackson, J. (ed) *Professions and Professionalisation*, Cambridge University Press: Cambridge.

Johnson, T.J. (1972), *Professions and Power*, Macmillan: London.

Jones, C. (1983), *State Social Work and the Working Class*, Macmillan: London.

Jones, C. and Novak, T. (1993), 'Social Work Today', *British Journal of Social Work*, 23, pp. 195-212.

Joyce, P., Corrigan, P. and Hayes, M. (1988), *Striking Out. Trade Unionism in Social Work*, Macmillan: Basingstoke.

Kelly, A. (1992), 'The New Managerialism in the Social Services', in Carter, P., Jeffs, T. and Smith, M. (eds) *Social Work and Social Welfare Yearbook 3, 1991*, Open University Press: Milton Keynes.

Kets de Vries M.F.R. (1980), *Organisational Paradoxes. Clinical Approaches to Management*, Tavistock: London.

Kirwan, M. (1994). 'Gender and Social Work: Will Dip.S.W. Make a Difference?', *British Journal of Social Work*, 24, pp.137-155.

Knights, D. and Willmott, H. (eds) (1986a), *Gender and the Labour Process*, Gower: Aldershot.

Knights, D. and Willmott, H. (eds) (1986b), *Managing the Labour Process*, Gower: Aldershot.

Knights, D., Willmott, H. and Collinson, D. (eds) (1985), *Job Redesign. Critical Perspectives on the Labour Process*, Gower: Aldershot.

Knights, D. and Willmott, H. (1989), 'Power and Subjectivity at Work: From Degradation to Subjugation in Social Relations', *Sociology*, 23, 4, pp. 535-558.

Kuhn, T. (1970), *The Structure of Scientific Revolutions*, University of Chicago Press: Chicago.

Laffin, M. and Young, K. (1990), *Professionalism in Local Government*, Longman: Harlow.

Langan, M. (1992), 'Introduction: Women and Social Work in the 1990s', in Langan, M. and Day, L. *Women, Oppression and Social Work*, Routledge: London.

Langan, M. (1993), 'The Rise and Fall of Social Work', in Clarke, J. (ed) *A Crisis in Care? Challenges to Social Work*, Sage: London.

Langan, M. and Clarke, J. (1994) 'Managing in the Mixed Economy of Care', in Clarke, J., Cochrane, A. and McLaughlin, E. (eds) (1994) *Managing Social Policy*, Sage: London.

Langan, M. and Day, L. (1992), *Women, Oppression and Social Work*, Routledge: London.

Langan, M. and Lee, P. (eds) (1989), *Radical Social Work Today*, Unwin Hyman: London.

Leach, S., Stewart, J. and Walsh, K. (1994), *The Changing Organisation and Management of Local Government*, Macmillan: Basingstoke.

Leeds Social Workers' Action Group (1983), 'Leeds Social Workers' Action Group', in Jordan, B. and Parton, N. (eds) *The Political Dimensions of Social Work*, Basil Blackwell: Oxford.

Leonard, P. (1975), 'Towards a Paradigm for Radical Practice', in Bailey, R. and Brake, M. *Radical Social Work*, Edward Arnold: London.

Lipsky, M. (1980), *Street-Level Bureaucracy*, Russell Sage: New York.

Littler, C.R. (1982), *The Development of the Labour Process in Capitalist Societies: A Comparative Analysis of Work Organisation in Britain, the USA and Japan*, Heinemann: London.

Littler, C.R. and Salaman, G. (1982), 'Bravermania and Beyond', *Sociology*, 16, 2, pp. 251-269.

Littler, C.R. and Salaman, G. (1984), *Class at Work*, Batsford: London.

Lockwood, D. (1958), *The Blackcoated Worker*, Allen and Unwin: London.

Mann, M. (1973), *Consciousness and Action Amongst the Western Working Class*, Macmillan: London.

Martin, J. and Roberts, C. (1984), *Women and Employment: A Lifetime Perspective*, HMSO: London.

Marquand, D. (1988), *The Unprincipled Society*, Fontana: London.

Marwick, A. (1990), *British Society Since 1945*, Penguin: London.

Marx, K. (1974), *Capital. Volume One*, Dent Dutton: London.

Massey, D. (1983), 'The Shape of Things to Come', *Marxism Today*, April.

Maud Report (1967), *Report of the Committee on Management in Local Government*, HMSO: London.

Maybin, R. (1980), 'N.A.L.G.O.: The New Unionism of Contemporary Britain', *Marxism Today*, January.

Mercer, D.E. and Weir, D.T. (1972), 'Attitudes to Work and Trade Unionism Amongst White Collar Workers', *Industrial Relations*, 3, pp. 54-71.

Mishra, R. (1984), *The Welfare State in Crisis*, Wheatsheaf: Brighton.

Mitchell, J.C. (1983), 'Case and Situation Analysis', *Sociological Review*, 31, pp. 187-211.

Morgan, G. and Hooper, D. (1987), 'Corporate Strategy, Ownership and Control', *Sociology*, 21, 4, pp. 609-627.

N.A.L.G.O. (1976), *Report of the Working Party on Communications*, N.A.L.G.O.: London.

Newman, J. (1994), 'The Limits of Management: Gender and the Politics of Change', in Clarke, J., Cochrane, A. and McLaughlin, E. (eds) *Managing Social Policy*, Sage: London..

Newman, J. and Clarke, J. (1994), 'Going about our Business? The Managerialisation of Public Services', in Clarke, J., Cochrane, A. and McLaughlin, E. (eds) *Managing Social Policy*, Sage: London.

Newman, J. and Clarke, J. (1997), *The Managerial State*, Sage: London.

Nichols, T. (ed) (1980), *Capital and Labour*, Fontana: Glasgow.

Nichols, T. and Beynon, H. (1977), *Living with Capitalism*, Routledge and Kegan Paul: London.

Nicholson, N., Bursell, G. and Blyton, P. (1981), *The Dynamics of White Collar Unionism*, Academic Press: London.

O'Connor, J. (1973), *The Fiscal Crisis of the State*, St. Martin's Press: New York.

Offe, C. (1975), 'The Theory of the Capitalist State and the Problem of Policy Formation', in Lindberg, et al (eds), *Stress and Contradiction in Modern Capitalism*, Heath Press: Lexington.

Offe, C. (1983), 'Some Contradictions of the Modern Welfare State', *Critical Social Policy*, 6, pp. 7-16.

O'Higgins, M. (1992), 'Effective Management: The Challenges', in Harding, T. (ed), *Who Owns Welfare? Questions on the Social Services Agenda*, Social Services Policy Forum Paper No.2., NISW: London.

Oppenheimer, M. (1975), 'The Proletarianisation of the Professional', in Halmos, P. (ed), *Professionalisation and Social Change*, Sociological Review Monograph No. 20.

Osmond, R. et al (1977), 'The Caseload Monitoring System', *Social Work Today*, 8, p. 16.

Packman, J., Randall, J. and Jacques, W. (1986), *Who Needs Care? Social Work Decisions about Children*, Basil Blackwell: Oxford.

Parry, N. and Parry, J. (1979), 'Social Work, Professionalism and the State', in Parry, N., Rustin, M. and Satyamurti, C. (eds), *Social Work Welfare and the State*, Edward Arnold: London.

Parsloe, P. (1981), *Social Services Area Teams*, George Allen and Unwin: London.

Parsloe, P. and Stevenson, O. (1978), *Social Services Teams: The Practitioners' View*, H.M.S.O.: London.

Payne, M. (1979), *Power, Authority and Responsibility in Social Services*, Macmillan: London.

Pearson, G. (1973), 'Social Work as the Privatised Solution to Public Ills', *British Journal of Social Work*, 3, 2, pp. 209-228.

Pearson, G. (1975), 'Making Social Workers: Bad Promises and Good Omens', in Bailey, R. and Brake, M. (eds), *Radical Social Work*, Edward Arnold: London.

Perrow, C. (1970), *Organisational Analysis: A Sociological View*, Tavistock: London.

Phillips, A. and Taylor, B. (1980), 'Sex and Skill: Notes Towards a Feminist Economics', *Feminist Review*, 6, pp. 79-88.

Philpot, T. (1985), 'Tom, Tom the Miner's Son', *Community Care*, 23rd May, pp. 15-18.

Pithouse, A. (1987), *Social Work: The Social Organisation of an Invisible Trade*, Gower: Aldershot.

Pithouse, A. (1991), 'Guardians of Autonomy: Work Orientations in a Social Work Office', in Carter, P., Jeffs, T. and Smith, S. (eds), *Social Work and Social Welfare Yearbook 2, 1990*, Open University Press: Milton Keynes.

Pollert, A. (1981), *Girls, Wives, Factory Lives*, Macmillan: London.

Pollitt, C. (1990), *Managerialism and the Public Services*, Basil Blackwell: Oxford.

Poulantzas, N. (1975), *Classes in Contemporary Capitalism*, New Left Books: London.

Prandy, K., Stewart, A. and Blackburn, R.M. (1982), *White Collar Work*, Macmillan: London.

Pugh, D. (1988), 'The Aston Research Programme', in Bryman, A. (ed), *Doing Research in Organisations*, Routledge: London.

Ramsay, H., Baldry, C., Connolly, A. and Lockyer, C. (1991), 'Municipal Microchips: The Computerised Labour Process in the Public Service Sector', in Smith, C. Knights, D. and Willmott, H. (eds), *White-Collar Work. The Non-Manual Labour Process*, Macmillan: Basingstoke.

Rose, M. and Jones, B. (1985), 'Managerial Strategy and Trade Union Responses in Work Reorganisation Schemes at Establishment Level', in Knights, D., Willmott, H. and Collinson, D. (eds), *Job Redesign. Critical Perspectives on the Labour Process*, Gower: Aldershot.

Roy, D. (1960), 'Banana Time: Job Satisfaction and Informal Interaction', *Human Organisation*, 18, 4, pp. 158-168.

Salaman, G. (1979), *Work Organisations: Control and Resistance*, Longman: London.

Salaman, G. (1986), *Working*, Ellis Horwood and Tavistock: Chichester.

Satyamurti, C. (1981), *Occupational Survival*, Basil Blackwell: Oxford.

Scase, R. and Goffee, R. (1989), *Reluctant Managers. Their Work and Lifestyles*, Unwin Hyman: London.

Seebohm, F. (Chair) (1968), *Report of the Committee on Local Authority and Allied Personal Social Services*, Cmnd. 3703, H.M.S.O.: London.

Seebohm, F. (1989), *Seebohm Twenty Years On. Three Stages in the Development of the Personal Social Services*, Policy Studies Institute: London.

Sharpe, S. (1984), *Double Identity: The Lives of Working Mothers*, Penguin: Harmondsworth.

Sibeon, R. (1991), *Towards a New Sociology of Social Work*, Avebury: Aldershot.

Siltanen, J. (1981), 'A Commentary on Theories of Female Wage Labour', in Cambridge Women's Studies Group (eds), *Women in Society*, Virago: London.

Silverman, D. (1970), *The Theory of Organisations*, Heinemann: London.

Simpkin, M. (1979, 1983 [2nd ed.]), *Trapped Within Welfare. Surviving Social Work*, Macmillan: London.

Smith, D. (1965), 'Front-line Organisation of a State Mental Hospital', *Administrative Quarterly*, 10, pp. 381-399.

Smith, G. (1979), *Social Work and the Sociology of Organisations*, R.K.P.: London.

Smith, J. (1972), Top Jobs in the Social Services', in Jones, K. (ed), *The Yearbook of Social Policy in Britain 1971*, R.K.P.: London.

Smith, G. (1981), 'Discretionary Decision-making in Social Work', in Adler, M. and Asquith, S., *Discretion and Welfare*, Heinemann: London.

Smith, C. Knights, D. and Willmott, H. (1991), *White-Collar Work. The Non-Manual Labour Process*, Macmillan: Basingstoke.

Spoor, A. (1967), *White Collar Union*, Heinemann: London.

Stanley, L. and Wise, S. (1983), *Breaking Out: Feminist Consciousness and Feminist Research*, R.K.P.:London.

Stark, D. (1980), 'Class Struggle and the Labour Process', *Theory and Society*, 9, 1, pp. 69-84.

Stevenson, O. (1989), *Age and Vulnerability*, Edward Arnold: London.

Stewart, A., Prandy, K. and Blackburn, R.M. (1980), *Social Stratification and Occupations*, Macmillan: London.

Stewart, J. (1983), *Local Government: The Conditions of Local Choice*, Allen and Unwin: London.

Stewart, J. (1989), 'The Changing Organisation and Management of Local Authorities', in Stewart, J. and Stoker, G. (eds), *The Future of Local Government*, Macmillan: London.

Stewart, J. (1992), 'Guidelines for Public Sector Management: Lessons not to be Learned from the Private Sector', in Carter, P., Jeffs, T. and Smith, M. (eds), *Changing Social Work and Welfare*, Open University Press: Buckingham.

Stinchcombe, A.L. (1965), 'Social Structure and Organisations', in March, J.G. (ed), *Handbook of Organisations*, McNally: Chicago.

Storey, J. (1983), *Managerial Prerogative and the Question of Control*, R.K.P.: London.

Storey, J. (1985), 'The Means of Management Control', *Sociology*, 19, 2, pp.193-211.

Storey, J. (1986), 'The Phoney War? New Office Technology: Organisation and Control', in Knights, D. and Willmott, H. (eds), *Managing the Labour Process*, Gower: Aldershot.

Strauss, A.L., Schatzman, L., Ehrlich, D., Bucher, R. and Sabshin, M. (1963), 'The Hospital as a Negotiated Order', in Freidson, E. (ed), *The Hospital in Modern Society*, Macmillan: New York.

Strauss, G. (1983), 'White Collar Unions are Different', in Hyman, R. and Price, R., *The New Working Class*, Macmillan: London.

Taylor, C. (1994), 'Is Gender Inequality in Social Work Management Relevant to Social Work Students?', *British Journal of Social Work*, 24, pp. 157-172.

Teulings, A. (1986), 'Managerial Labour Processes in Organised Capitalism: The Power of Corporate Management and the Powerlessness of the Manager', in Knight, D. and Willmott, H. (eds), *Managing the Labour Process*, Gower: Aldershot.

Thomas, N. (1973), 'The Seebohm Committee on Personal Social Services', in Chapman, R.A. (ed), *The Role of Commissions in Policy Making*, Allen and Unwin: London.

Thompson, P. (1983), *The Nature of Work*, Macmillan: Basingstoke.

Thompson, P. and McHugh, D. (1990), *Work Organisations. A Critical Introduction*, Macmillan: Basingstoke.

Toren, N. (1972), *Social Work. The Case of a Semi-profession*, Sage: London.

Vickery, A. (1977), *Caseload Management*, National Institute for Social Work: London.

Volker, D. (1966), 'N.A.L.G.O.'s Affiliation to the TUC', *British Journal of Industrial Relations*, March 1966, pp. 13-24.

Wacjman, J. (1983), *Women in Control*, Open University Press: Milton Keynes.

Walby, S. (1986), *Patriarchy at Work: Patriarchal and Capitalist Relations in Employment*, Polity Press: Cambridge.

Webb, A. and Wistow, G. (1987), *Social Work, Social Care and Social Planning: The Personal Social Services Since Seebohm*, Longman: Harlow.

West, J. (ed) (1982), *Work, Women and the Labour Market*, Routledge and Kegan Paul: London.

Westwood, S. (1984), *All Day Every Day : Factory and Family in the Making of Women's Lives*, Pluto: London.

Whitmore, R. and Fuller, R. (1980), Priority Planning in an Area Social Service Team', *British Journal of Social Work*, 10, 3, pp. 352-371.

Whittington, R. (1988), 'Environmental Structure and Theories of Strategic Choice', *Journal of Management Studies*, 25, 6, pp. 521-536.

Wilding, P. (1982), *Professional Power and Social Welfare*, R.K.P.: London.

Williams, F. (1991), 'The Welfare State as Part of a Racially Structured and Patriarchal Capitalism', in Loney, M., Bocock, R., Clarke, J., Cochrane, A., Graham, P. and Wilson, M., *The State or the Market. Politics and Welfare in Contemporary Britain*, Sage: London.

Williams, F. (1993), 'Gender, "Race" and Class in British Welfare Policy', in Cochrane, A. and Clarke, J. (eds), *Comparing Welfare States. Britain in International Context*, Sage: London.

Willmott, H. (1989), 'Subjectivity and the Dialectics of Praxis: Opening up the Core of Labour Process Analysis', in Knights, D. and Willmott, H. (eds), *Labour Process Theory*, Macmillan: London.

Witz, A. (1990), 'Patriarchy and the Professions: The Gendered Politics of Occupational Closure', *Sociology*, 24, 4, pp. 675-690.

Witz, A. (1992), *Professions and Patriarchy*, Routledge: London.

Wood, S. (ed) (1982), *The Degradation of Work: Skill, De-skilling and the Labour Process*, Hutchison: London.

Wood, S. (ed) (1989), *The Transformation of Work? Skill, Flexibility and the Labour Process*, Unwin Hyman: London.

Wood, S. and Kelly, J. (1982), 'Taylorism, Responsible Autonomy and Management Strategy', in Wood S. (ed), *The Degradation of Work: Skill, De-skilling and the Labour Process*, Hutchison: London.

Wright Mills, C. (1959), *The Sociological Imagination*, Oxford University Press: New York.

Yin, R.K. (1984), *Case Study Research*, Sage: Beverly Hills.

Zimbalist, A. (ed) (1979), *Case Studies on the Labor Process*, Monthly Review Press: New York.